DIVERSITY WITHOUT DISCRIMINATION

Praise for Carol Swain's and Mike Towle's Work on DEI and Affirmative Action

"This timely book by Carol Swain, written at a pivotal moment in this history, unmasks these programs (DEI and affirmative action) in beautiful prose and, most importantly, tells us what we should do next in this country that truly recognizes the sacred promise that all men are indeed created equal."
— **James Lindsay,** PhD., Author, Mathematician, Self-proclaimed professional troublemaker, Founder of New Discourses, and Co-Author (Helen Pluckrose) of *Cynical Theories: How Activist Scholarship Made Everything about Race, Gender, and Identity—and Why This Harms Everybody*

"Carol Swain's unusual background and accomplishments make her uniquely qualified to speak with authority on issues involving identity politics. Her co-authored book is a thought-provoking treatise that seeks unity around one of the most contentious issues of our day. She is my hero."
— **Arthur B. Laffer,** PhD, American Economist

"The Supreme Court's ruling against affirmative action has intensified challenges to diversity, equity, and inclusion (DEI) initiatives. Here, Dr. Carol Swain, a longtime critic of DEI programs, and co-author Mike Towle elaborate on the case against them and offer fresh ideas on achieving just racial progress. A vital perspective for all who wish to understand the full range of views in today's racial policy debates."
— **Rogers Smith,** Christopher H. Browne Distinguished Emeritus Professor of Political Science, University of Pennsylvania

"This book is a must-read for anyone who is a student of free speech, or who is seeking an in-depth understanding of the cultural battle lines being drawn today between freedom and forced adherence to the droning mantra of DEI. So many speakers on this topic take a curse to the darkness approach. Swain and Towle present a refreshingly intellectual discussion of alternative solutions to the growing problem of woke indoctrination."
— **Larry Crain,** Author and Constitutional Lawyer

Praise for *The Adversity of Diversity*, the original version of this book

"Dr. Carol M. Swain and Mike Towle provide real insight into how the Left has hijacked diversity and injected woke indoctrination into all aspects of society. Anyone who believes in treating our fellow Americans in a fair and equitable manner should read this book."
— **U.S. Senator Marsha Blackburn**, Tennessee

"Carol Swain has a unique ability to help us see what is true, right and good in diversity, equity, and inclusion conversations. I recommend this book to all who desire a path forward in the very confusing landscape around these issues. Her perspective is one that I trust."
— **Bobby Harrington**, D. Min., CEO RENEW.org and Discipleship.org, Lead Pastor, Harpeth Christian Church

"Any member of a disadvantaged or underrepresented community seeking a role model for how to achieve the American dream should ditch their sense of entitlement, quit waiting on the government for a free ride, and follow the lead of Dr. Carol Swain, whose own path to success has been a true inspiration."
— **Robert L. Woodson**, Founder and President of the Woodson Center, 1776 Unites, and Voices of Black Mothers United

"In their groundbreaking book, Carol M. Swain and Mike Towle challenge the status quo of diversity, equity, and inclusion (DEI) practices. With keen insights and extensive research, they delve into the interplay between affirmative action, DEI, and critical race theory, providing a thought-provoking analysis that will reshape the conversation. This book offers a bold and compelling vision for achieving genuine unity in our workplaces and institutions."
— **Dr. Robert J. Pacienza,** Senior Pastor of Coral Ridge Presbyterian Church, President of D. James Kennedy Ministries

DIVERSITY WITHOUT DISCRIMINATION

How to Promote a Culture of Unity
in a Post-DEI/Affirmative Action World

Carol M. Swain

Carol M. Swain, PhD and Mike Towle

Foreword by Alan M. Dershowitz

Copyright©2023, 2025 by Carol M. Swain
All rights reserved. Written permission must be secured from the publisher or the authors to use or reproduce any part of this book, except for brief quotations in critical reviews or articles.

Diversity without Discrimination is an updated edition of the book originally titled *The Adversity of Diversity*, which was published in 2023.

ISBN: 978-1-7374198-7-7

Cover design by Lillian Abernathy
Cover photo by fizkes licensed through Shutterstock
Back cover photo of Carol Swain by Kevin Wimpy
Page layout by Win-Win Words LLC.

Dr. Carol Swain's March 23, 2023, Statement to the Texas Legislature on Senate Bill 16 (diversity, equity, and inclusion [DEI] and critical race theory [CRT] in higher education) is available upon request. Contact her at info@carolmswain.com

Personalized copies of *Diversity without Discrimination* can be ordered in bulk through Logos Books, logosnashville@gmail.com

Join the effort to help Reclaim America by making a tax-deductible contribution to Be the People Non-Profit, a 501c (3) that educates the public about the cultural, social, and economic issues of our day, https://bethepeoplenonprofit.com/

Printed in the United States of America

To America's children. I want my great-grandchildren Hezekiah, Heavenly, and Haevyn to grow up in a world where they are neither advantaged nor disadvantaged because of their skin color. Likewise, Jackson, Olivia, and Karis are white children I know and love who should bear no additional burden because of their skin color. What should ultimately matter is the content of their character.
— **Carol M. Swain**

To Andrew, for your support and inspiration.
— **Mike Towle**

Contents

	Foreword: Alan M. Dershowitz	xi
	Preface: A New Dawn for Unity and Merit	xiii
	Acknowledgments	xvii
1	Trump's DEI Deathblow: Affirmative Action's Final Curtain	1
2	Carol's Educational Journey in an Affirmative Action-Infused World	17
3	Diversity Training: A Corporate Conundrum That's Resolving Itself	31
4	A Not-So-Inconvenient Death: The Martyrdom of George Floyd	43
5	DEI Training and Its Descent into Divisiveness	57
6	REAL Unity Training Solutions: An Antidote to DEI's Divisiveness	71
	Epilogue: The Shifting Sands of DEI and Affirmative Action Since July 2023	85
	Notes	89
	Appendix A: Executive Orders on DEI and Affirmative Action by President Donald J. Trump, January 20-21, 2025	103
	Appendix B: 14th Amendment to the U.S. Constitution	117
	Author Bios	119

Foreword

THE SUPREME COURT'S 2023 DECISION to declare race-based affirmative action in higher education unconstitutional marked a watershed moment. Now, with President Trump's executive orders on January 20-21, 2025—"Ending Radical and Wasteful Government DEI Programs" and "Ending Illegal Discrimination and Restoring Merit-Based Opportunity"—we've taken a giant leap forward. Carol M. Swain's *Diversity without Discrimination*, an update to her work with Mike Towle, *The Adversity of Diversity*, lands at the perfect juncture. It's a passionate call for Americans to accept the end of Diversity, Equity, and Inclusion (DEI) initiatives and instead shift toward loftier goals that can unite Americans around shared values.

Swain and Towle argue persuasively that DEI and race-based affirmative action—both swept away by Trump's decisive orders—ran afoul of the Civil Rights Act of 1964 and the Fourteenth Amendment's Equal Protection Clause. Instead of knitting us together, these policies often deepened divides, putting group labels ahead of individual worth. The authors' solution? A return to nondiscrimination, equal opportunity, and a merit-driven approach that reflects the Civil Rights Movement's heart. It's a stance I've echoed since the 1970s, when I urged affirmative action to focus on economic need and personal drive over race alone.

I've long admired efforts to give underrepresented strivers a shot at a good education—doors opened with good intent. Swain's own journey from rural Virginia poverty to academic heights shows what's possible when opportunity meets effort. Her vision resonates with me, even if we might differ on some details. The Court's ruling, and now Trump's orders, are wins I've sought for more than fifty years. As a Jewish son of Eastern European stock, I knew discrimination's sting—graduating first in my Yale Law class in the '60s, only to be iced out by all thirty-two Wall Street firms I applied to. My clothing was not the problem. That sort of discrimination fired my civil rights zeal, from '60s marches to standing in awe as Dr. Martin Luther King Jr. dreamed of character trumping color.

But the fight's not over. Swain notes the lawsuits stacking up against Trump's orders—DEI holdouts like the National Association of Diversity Officers scrambling to prop up their fading regime. They're on shaky ground. The law stands firm for equality, not identity games. With DEI crumbling—job postings off from their peak by 2023, diversity chiefs cut loose, and McKinsey's profit boasts unmasked as thin air—the momentum is on the side of real equality. This isn't a setback; it's a breakthrough.

Some schools and firms might still dodge the rules, chasing "racial justice" shadows despite the Court. It'll take watchdogs and legal muscle to keep them honest. I'd go a step beyond Swain: axe legacy admits, athletic edges, and other merit-blind perks, too. Let's level the field fully, honoring King's vision and the Constitution's promise.

Swain's celebrating DEI's end, not mourning it, and I'm raising a glass with her. Her book sketches a path to diversity without discrimination, rooted in America's finest ideals: fairness, effort, and unity over fracture. It's a compelling case, worth wrestling with even if you don't sign every line. I've seen brilliance across every race and creed—talent knows no bounds. This is our moment to build a nation that proves it. Let's get to it.

— **Alan M. Dershowitz**
Felix Frankfurter Professor of Law (emeritus) at Harvard University Law School, and author of numerous bestselling books, including *The Case for Color-Blind Equality in an Age of Identity Politics*.

Preface:
A New Dawn for Unity and Merit

WELCOME TO A BOLD NEW CHAPTER IN AMERICA'S STORY—a chapter where we finally shed the divisive baggage of Diversity, Equity, and Inclusion (DEI) programs and affirmative action, and embrace a future rooted in nondiscrimination, equal opportunity, merit, and fairness. These values will lead us to a unified society in which people are not dismissed and stepped over because of some immutable characteristic. If you're expecting a funeral dirge for the end of these policies, you've come to the wrong place. This isn't a time to mourn; it's a time to celebrate.[1] On January 20-21, 2025, President Donald J. Trump signed two executive orders—"Ending Radical and Wasteful Government DEI Programs" and "Ending Illegal Discrimination and Restoring Merit-Based Opportunity"—that turned the page on six decades of race- and sex-based preferences masquerading as progress and opened the door to true equality under the law.[2] And let me tell you, it's about time.

I'm not here to bury the past but to plant seeds for a brighter future. As a black woman born into abject poverty in rural Virginia, a high school dropout, and teen wife and mother who went on to earn five college and university degrees, I've lived the promise of the Civil Rights Movement. The Civil Rights Act of 1964, the Voting Rights Act of 1965, and the Open Housing Act of 1968 didn't just open doors; they kicked them wide open for people like me.[3] Those laws, grounded in the Equal Protection Clause of the Fourteenth Amendment, gave me a shot at the American Dream based on my grit and willingness to work hard and take advantage of opportunities that came my way. I seized that chance, and it changed my life.

So when I say the death of DEI and affirmative action takes us back to those principles of nondiscrimination and equal opportunity, I mean it as the highest compliment. We're not retreating; we're reclaiming what worked for everyone.

For too long, DEI and affirmative action twisted that noble legacy into a racial and gender spoils system that undermined everything for which the Civil Rights Movement fought. Instead of equality under the law of the Civil Rights Act of 1964, passed by Congress, we got quotas, preferences, and a culture obsessed with checking boxes instead of building bridges. President Trump's eight-page directive nailed it: these policies saddled our institutions with "dangerous, demeaning, and immoral race- and sex-based preferences" that corroded national unity and devalued "hard work, excellence, and individual achievement."[4] In fields such as medicine, aviation, and law enforcement, DEI even lowered standards, putting public safety at risk. That's not progress—it's a betrayal of the American promise.

But here's the good news: the end of this era isn't a loss—it's a liberation. We're free now to build something better, a culture of unity that celebrates diversity without mandating discrimination. This new book, *Diversity without Discrimination*, an update of my co-authored book *The Adversity of Diversity*, is your roadmap to that future. It's not about erasing differences but about honoring them through a shared commitment to merit and fairness. And trust me, we've got the tools to make it happen—tools forged centuries ago by men and women of integrity who believed in our nation's Judeo-Christian roots. More than sixty years ago, Americans came together around a vision of civil rights that emphasized nondiscrimination and equal opportunity. Working together across racial, ethnic, and partisan lines, a motley crew of Americans and committed activists from around the world helped our nation move forward in a powerful and lasting manner.

THE DEI MIRAGE: A HOUSE OF CARDS COLLAPSES

Let's rewind a bit. After George Floyd's tragic death in 2020, corporate America jumped onto the DEI bandwagon with both feet. Billions of dollars were poured into initiatives, grants, and loans to fight "racial injustice"—$50 billion in pledges by August 2020 alone.[5] Chief diversity officers sprouted up like mushrooms, and by 2021, 94 percent of new jobs at S&P 100 companies went to people of color.[6] Activists cheered, consultants

Preface: A New Dawn for Unity and Merit

cashed in, and firms such as McKinsey & Company churned out studies claiming DEI boosted profits.[7] It was a gold rush of good intentions.

Then the cracks appeared. By 2023, the shine was off. DEI job postings plummeted—down 44 percent from their peak, with a 23 percent drop that November alone.[8] Companies quietly started axing their diversity czars, and the Supreme Court's ruling against race-based college admissions that same year only accelerated the retreat.[9] Why the collapse? Because DEI never delivered. For all its promises of harmony and profitability, it sowed conflict, alienated workers, and failed every rigorous test of its claims. When researchers Jeremiah Green and John Hand dug into McKinsey's data, they found it unreliable—unreproducible junk science dressed up as gospel.[10] Corporate America finally noticed.

DEI's fatal flaw was simple: it broke the law and the spirit of 1964. As I argued in my previous book, *The Adversity of Diversity,* these programs violated the Civil Rights Act and the Fourteenth Amendment by favoring some groups over others.[11] Affirmative action devolved into reverse discrimination—against white males, Asians, Christians, conservatives, you name it—while DEI turned workplaces and campuses into battlegrounds of resentment. It wasn't unity; it was division with a fancier name.

LAWFARE'S LAST GASP: THE OLD GUARD FIGHTS BACK

Of course, the old guard isn't going quietly. As I write this on March 15, 2025, dozens of lawsuits are piling up against Trump's executive orders.[12] Groups such as the National Association of Diversity Officers in Higher Education and the mayor of Baltimore are crying foul, claiming the EOs violate free speech and due process.[13] It's lawfare déjà vu—straight out of the playbook that failed to stop Trump's reelection. Spoiler alert: it's not going to work this time either.

Why? Because the law is on our side. The Civil Rights Act and the Constitution don't bend for identity politics—they demand equality, period. DEI's defenders can't square their race-based schemes with nondiscrimination, and the courts know it. The momentum is with Trump's vision to "Make America Great Again" by rooting out waste and restoring merit. Americans are tired of the same old song and dance—Jean-Baptiste Alphonse Karr's "the more things change, the more they stay the same" doesn't have to be our fate.[14] We're ready for real change.

A VISION OF UNITY: DIVERSITY DONE RIGHT

So what does a post-DEI world look like? Not a monochrome dystopia dominated by privileged white males—let's put that scare tactic to rest. Our anti-discrimination laws, battle-tested since 1964, will ensure a vibrant mix of talent and perspectives. However, it will not guarantee the equity (equal results) sought by the DEI crowd, nor should it. DEI is DOA—dead on arrival. Diversity isn't the enemy; discrimination is. And without DEI's heavy hand, we can achieve the former without the latter.

Picture this: companies adopt public schools in struggling neighborhoods, offering mentorship and skills training to children of all backgrounds. Job fairs pop up in high-unemployment areas, open to anyone with the drive to show up. Colleges focus on outreach that's race- and gender-neutral, tapping into the God-given ingenuity that's spread across every group. It's not utopia—it's America at its best, trusting in merit and opportunity to lift us all.

I've seen it work. Civil rights laws didn't just save me—they unleashed a generation of strivers who proved talent knows no color or creed. We don't need DEI's crutches or affirmative action's handouts. We need a level playing field and a culture that cheers hard work over handouts. That's the unity we've been chasing all along.

HOPE ON THE HORIZON

This book isn't a lament—it's a rallying cry. The end of DEI and affirmative action isn't the death of diversity; it's the birth of something stronger. We're not erasing the past but building on its best parts. The Civil Rights Movement gave us the foundation; now it's our turn to raise the roof. In these pages, you'll find stories, strategies, and a vision for a nation where unity isn't a slogan—it's a reality.

So turn the page with me. Let's celebrate the end of a divisive era and step boldly into one where every American gets a fair shot—not because of their identity, but because of their effort. The future's bright, and it's ours to build. Ready? Let's go.

Acknowledgments

A SPECIAL THANKS TO BRENDA GILCHRIST OF HRMATRIX, Molly Bolen of IngramSpark, co-author and editor Mike Towle, friend and sounding board Donna Willis, and my executive assistant, Sandy Norris for their advice, insights, and encouragement every step of the way. As always, I give thanks to God and the faith community worldwide that undergirds me with their prayers and words of encouragement.

DIVERSITY WITHOUT DISCRIMINATION

CHAPTER 1

Trump's DEI Deathblow: Affirmative Action's Final Curtain

"You do not take a person who, for years, has been hobbled by chains and liberate him, bring him up to the starting line of a race and then say, 'You are free to compete with all the others,' and still justly believe that you have been completely fair. . .

"This is the next and the more profound stage of the battle for civil rights. We seek not just freedom but opportunity. We seek not just legal equity but human ability, not just equality as a right and a theory but equality as a fact and equality as a result."[1]
— **President Lyndon Baines Johnson,** Howard University Commencement Address, June 4, 1965.

Fifty-eight years later:
"[W]hat cannot be done directly cannot be done indirectly. The Constitution deals with substance, not shadows," and the prohibition against racial discrimination is "leveled at the thing, not the name." . . . A benefit to a student who overcame racial discrimination, for example, must be tied to that student's courage and determination. Or a benefit to a student whose heritage or culture motivated him or her to assume a leadership role or attain a particular goal must be tied to that student's unique ability to contribute to the university. In other words, the student must be treated based on his or her experiences as an individual—not on the basis of race. Many universities have for too long done

just the opposite. And in doing so, they have concluded, wrongly, that the touchstone of an individual's identity is not challenges bested, skills built, or lessons learned but the color of their skin. Our constitutional history does not tolerate that choice."[2]

> — **U.S. Supreme Court Chief Justice John Roberts**, Majority Opinion, *Students for Fair Admissions v. President and Fellows of Harvard College*, June 29, 2023.

TRADITIONAL UNDERSTANDINGS OF EQUALITY AND JUSTICE are making a triumphant return in America, driven by President Donald Trump's bold moves in his first few days of his second term. On January 20-21, 2025, Trump issued several executive orders that delivered a fatal blow to Diversity, Equity, and Inclusion (DEI) initiatives and more than six decades of affirmative action, ending race-based preferences in federal workplaces and contracting.[3] As of March 21, 2025, however, most media commentators seem to have missed the significance of the later, more far-reaching EOs.

These orders dismantled policies tracing back to the 1960s, when President John F. Kennedy's Executive Order 10925 first directed federal contractors to ensure equal treatment "without regard to race, creed, color, religion, or national origin,"[4] a mandate later expanded by President Lyndon B. Johnson's 1965 and 1967 orders linking civil rights to affirmative action and adding sex as a protected category.[5] Not to be left behind, Richard Nixon earned his place in history as the first Republican to shape these policies. In 1969, Nixon amended Johnson's order, pledging to "promote the full realization of equal employment opportunity through a continuing affirmative program in each executive department and agency."[6] Through the Philadelphia Plan, Nixon introduced Americans to "goals and timetables" that soon evolved into outright quotas.[7]

Trump's first order, signed January 20, 2025, banned race-based hiring and promotion in federal agencies, terminating DEI programs and enforcing merit-based standards. His second EO, issued January 21, 2025, rescinded all prior affirmative action-related executive orders, including Kennedy's EO 10925 and Johnson's EO 11246, erasing their legal footing. These orders effectively bar federal contractors from using DEI criteria and instead follow mandates in compliance with anti-discrimination laws and prioritize merit over demographics. Complementing these, Trump signed Executive Order 14168 on January 20, 2025, titled "Defending Women from Gender Ideology

Extremism and Restoring Biological Truth to the Federal Government," which reinforced women's rights by defining sex as an immutable binary—male and female—based on biology at conception.[8] This order prohibited federal recognition of gender identity, ended funding for gender-affirming care, and mandated that government documents like passports reflect biological sex, aiming to protect single-sex spaces and sports for women. Together, these actions signal the final curtain for affirmative action and a reassertion of traditional equality rooted in merit and biology.

BRIEF HISTORICAL OVERVIEW OF AFFIRMATIVE ACTION

John F. Kennedy's 1961 Executive Order 10925, directed at federal contractors and described above, had the most conspicuous impact and brought the term "affirmative action" into the American lexicon. This was before the passage of the Civil Rights Act of 1964 that prohibited discrimination based on race, color, religion, sex, or national origin. Kennedy's EO became the law of the land when Congress passed the Civil Rights Act of 1964. A year later, before the new Civil Rights Law had had time to be fully implemented, Johnson gave his famous Howard University commencement speech that used the metaphor of a shackled runner to make the case for racial and ethnic preferences. Johnson articulated a vision for addressing racial inequality that went beyond legal equality, laying the intellectual groundwork for affirmative action by emphasizing the need for "equality as a fact and equality as a result." Following this speech, he issued Executive Order 11246 on September 24, 1965, which established affirmative action requirements for federal contractors.

Sociologist John D. Skrentny has explained the shift from civil rights enforcement to preferential treatment as emanating from the situation of crisis management that followed in the wake of urban riots that began in the summer of 1963 and culminated in 1967. According to Skrentny, it was white male elites who pressed for more aggressive methods to quicken the pace of progress.[9]

In response to the riots, President Johnson issued EO 11365 establishing the National Advisory Commission on Civil Rights that became known as the Kerner Commission. It concluded: "Our nation is moving toward two societies, one black, one white—separate and unequal." The report was a strong indictment of white America: "What white Americans have never fully understood—

but what the Negro can never forget—is that white society is deeply implicated in the ghetto. White institutions created it, white institutions maintain it, and white society condones it."[10]

AFFIRMATIVE ACTION: NEVER ACTUAL LAW IN TRADITIONAL SENSE

For decades, affirmative action was widely treated (or feared) as if it were law. In reality, affirmative action had neither been created by legislation—i.e., voted on by Congress and signed into law by a sitting president—nor had it been added as an amendment to the U.S. Constitution. What affirmative action had going for it was the power and influence of the civil rights movement of the 1960s. That movement yielded the watershed Civil Rights Act of 1964 but also organized hordes of loyal, sharp-elbowed activists who aggressively pushed affirmative action and were never shy about getting into the faces (or inside the heads) of anyone reluctant to go along with their program.

I (Carol) was a ten-year-old black girl living in the rural South when President Johnson signed the Civil Rights Act of 1964 into law. The Civil Rights Act prohibited government-sanctioned discrimination based on race, color, national origin, sex, or religion. It was seismic in its impact because it banned segregation in movie theaters, restaurants, and hotels. It meant that people like me were no longer barred from using public swimming pools or libraries, and it mandated that states not in compliance with the 1954 *Brown v. Board of Education* of Topeka, Kansas, ruling had to stop dragging their feet.

LBJ's 1965 Howard University speech referenced above was significant because it signaled that the federal government would use racial preferences to achieve equal results or in today's language, equity (equal outcomes). Affirmative action would use racial preferences to address the past and present effects of discrimination against the black descendants of slaves. In doing so, affirmative action contradicted the words spoken by the floor manager of the legislation, Minnesota Senator Hubert Humphrey. He vowed that the legislation would not lead to racial preference or quotas, and that if it someone could find where it did, he would "start eating the pages" of the bill. We assume he never did.

What started off as path-breaking civil rights law that brought Americans together across racial, political, and religious lines was quickly neutralized by Johnson's affirmative action EO. Initially, the nation focused on outreach, nondiscrimination, equal opportunity, and integration as the instruments for diversifying workplaces and educational institutions. Affirmative action soon became about goals and timetables and more aggressive actions to pursue a form of diversity that could bring about integration of women and minorities into places where both groups had been shut out. There is some data to suggest that white women have always been the greatest beneficiaries of DEI and affirmative action programs.[11] Over the course of six decades affirmative action became more closely intertwined with diversity goals that morphed into DEI programs. What we had in America prior to the Trump EOs, which have thrown everything into flux, was a form of DEI best described as affirmative action on steroids.

Words have lost their meanings, and integrationist goals have become verboten. By 2025, DEI was not about integration and equal opportunity. It had become something more disturbing. The "D" in DEI now stood for Diversity, but diversity was no longer about integrating racial and ethnic minorities into institutions where they have been underrepresented. It was now about recruiting members of historically marginalized groups and empowering them to maintain their separate identities. DEI's diversity is based on a conflict model of human relations obsessed with differences and grievances about real and imagined historical wrongs.

The "E" in DEI stood for Equity, but equity was not about nondiscrimination and treating people fairly. Nor was it about ensuring equal opportunity. Instead, it was about ensuring equal outcomes based on group membership. Equity became a key demand of critical race theory proponents. They sought equal outcomes for protected groups describe as historically disadvantaged regardless of their efforts, talents, or abilities.

The "I" in DEI stood for Inclusion. Inclusion was not just about integrating people into institutions and areas of life where they were previously excluded. It was about allowing them to maintain and celebrate their differences. That is the opposite of what the word *inclusion* implies. DEI blocked the path to unity because it opposed assimilation, merit, and integration. It embraced group differences and was at war with heterosexuality, the white race ("whiteness"), and core American values such as equal treatment under the law.

The hullabaloo about DEI was always misplaced and misguided. Affirmative action and DEI share a common DNA with the equal opportunity movement that gained significant traction in the 1970s. Both are entrenched as practitioners and promoters of reverse discrimination. This is particularly true of DEI, which has shown significantly more bite than affirmative action in brazenly putting Whites, especially white males, on notice about their guilt for the nearly 250 years of alleged "sins" committed by America's founding fathers and their descendants.

Until the second election of Donald J. Trump, not a single U.S. president (not even the staunchly conservative Ronald Reagan)—there had been ten presidential terms since Nixon—had had the courage to issue an EO overturning Johnson's executive order even though everyone knew that it changed and in some ways nullified key protections guaranteed to all Americans based on the Civil Rights Act of 1964 and the Equal Protection Clause of the Fourteenth Amendment. Affirmative action was the five-hundred-pound gorilla sitting in the middle of the room pounding its chest until DEI and CRT sucked the air from the room.

PROGRESSIVES AND REVERSE DISCRIMINATION

Unfortunately, America seems besieged by radical "progressives" intent on ignoring the Equal Protection cCause of the Fourteenth Amendment and the Civil Rights Act of 1964 and its amendments. After Trump issued his EO that overturned Johnson's EO establishing affirmative action, some Americans are intent on pretending like nothing has changed. They act like it is business as usual. They express these sentiments by openly defying President Trump's EO and vowing to continue the good fight by pushing what is divisive DEI training programs that are wedded to Marxist-driven philosophies and tactics of extremist groups like Black Lives Matter (BLM), antifa, and the National Education Association. We have reached a point where the Marxist-influenced "progressives" that control many college and university campuses have put critical race theory, political correctness, wokeism, and cancel culture into a blender and mixed them all together, served cold in how they undermine traditional American freedoms, thought, and culture. They do this by promoting reverse discrimination, deterring free speech in part by silencing dissenting voices (with help from Big Media, such as Facebook, and, at one time, X [formerly known as Twitter]). It seems as if these gatekeepers who act as if they are the ruling class born to control the rubes take great delight in devaluing the citizenship dignity of whites and conservative minorities. When dealing with white Americans we often see them tossing out false, incendiary labels such as "White privilege" and "White supremacy," as well as blanket accusations of

Trump's DEI Deathblow: Affirmative Action's Final Curtain

Whites being "racist" at birth. This is not a joke, but it is a mess.

DEI has failed miserably. It probably would have been more effective (at worst tolerable) if businesses and colleges treated their programs less like chasing a cure for cancer and more like an honest pursuit of healing the racial/ethnic divide eating away at America's soul. Unlike the traditional diversity measures once associated with affirmative action, DEI is more witch hunt than warm heart, more command and control than compromise and conciliation. DEI and affirmative action could never bring about a unified America because the premises undergirding the policies were flawed.

I (Mike) see DEI as a progressives-driven "front." It is the clichéd dry-cleaning shop hiding the operation that manufactures reverse discrimination to support the far-Left liberal cause. Diversity training is predicated on a Marxist-driven lie known as White oppression and Black victimization, which are foundational to critical race theory and the DEI action-driven enforcement arm. DEI is a rallying cry for BLM proponents who take pleasure in painting white people as inherently privileged and innately racist, although white progressives attempt to dodge such labels for themselves by adopting and parroting the lines of the activists. As a white man, I wonder how white progressives reconcile themselves with these prejudicial beliefs. White progressives should be their own worst enemies—because their skin color, alone, by their own declarations, make them purveyors of White privilege and White supremacy. Explain that.

Here's the stark truth about DEI: Diversity programs and those who enacted them have generally failed to make their workplaces more diverse, even while pandering to minorities (and alienating Whites). In fact, most diversity programs have failed to increase diversity, period. That's in large part because, since the 1970s, companies have switched to oppressive strategies such as diversity training to reduce bias, hiring tests and performance ratings connected to hires and promotions, and grievance systems to help employees call out managers for unacceptable behaviors (i.e., bias in the workplace). These dated practices, Dobbin and Kaley say, cobble an environment of "force-feeding" that promotes bias more than squelches it.[12]

It's not just the failures in achieving desired diversity numbers, either; there are also DEI systemic abuses (i.e., attempted cheating) that along the way have proven costly for companies and organizations. Such instances include firing white employees for apparently bogus reasons, and then hiring minority replacements as a quick and easy boost to their diversity numbers. This gives a whole new perspective to "cooking the books."

David Duvall is a former senior vice president of marketing and communications for North Carolina-based Novant Health, a nonprofit health care organization of thirty-five thousand employees scattered across many states. Without warning, and despite lacking a paper trail proving that Duvall had been warned about what was later revealed as alleged subpar work performance, Novant fired Duvall, a white male, in July 2018. They then ordered him off the premises immediately and reportedly hired two minorities—a white woman and a black woman—to split duties in sharing Duvall's former workload.[13]

Duvall filed a federal lawsuit claiming that Novant had violated the Civil Rights Act of 1964 by firing him to achieve racial and gender diversity. Despite the insistence by Novant's legal representation that Duvall had actually been terminated due to job performance, which Novant claimed was not indicative of the caliber of leadership someone in his position needed, the jury sided with Duvall. He was awarded $10 million in punitive damages in October 2021. Duvall's court documents also revealed that other white men at Novant had been fired without warning and replaced by minorities, including women.[14]

S. Luke Largesse, Duvall's attorney, said that his client's lawsuit was not an indictment of the existence of diversity and inclusion programs. He added, "The lawsuit was only about the need to run such programs lawfully. We believe the punitive damages award was a strong message that an employer cannot just fire employees based on their race or gender to create opportunities to achieve diversity targets. That is plainly unlawful and very harmful, and that is what the jury denounced here."[15]

DIVERSITY: A LIFE OF ITS OWN

Diversity is no longer just a nice word depicting a workplace organically composed of a variety of races, ethnicities, faiths, and gender identifications. The word has taken on a life of its own; it represents an obsession gripping our nation, a concession to the PC police. The idea of *diversity* represents the key ingredient in identity politics—if you identify as someone who fits into a highly sought-after diversity demographic (for example, a trans woman such as Dylan Mulvaney), then you suddenly had a huge advantage in the DEI environment. In sports, for example, there's the biological male at birth who switches genders—or even just gender identification—and suddenly gains an enormous competitive advantage participating in events against nontrans girls or women. Case in point is transgender athlete Lia Thomas, who in 2022 won an NCAA Division I swimming championship competing in the women's division[16]—and who sometime soon after was photographed wearing an antifa T-shirt. This is progress? No, not quite.

Trump's dealt blow to DEI includes an effort to end the practice of men competing in women's sports. On February 5, 2025, Trump issued an EO aimed at keeping men out of women's sports. Colleges and universities found in violation of the EO could lose significant funding totaling millions of dollars.[17] Although much progress has been made in some states with regard to preventing men (trans women) from participating in women's sports, there are frontiers where this battle has not been won.

One particular area concerns men who pledge into women's sororities where they expect full acceptance for their desire to join the sisterhood. In 2015, Kappa Kappa Gamma's Fraternity Council changed its rules to open membership for men who identify as women. By 2023, the alumnae had had enough. Patsy Levang and Cheryl Tuck-Smith, alumnae of more than fifty years, expressed their disapproval and were kicked out of the organization because of their support of a lawsuit challenging Kappa Kappa's unilateral policy decision to open the organization to men and fast track males for leadership positions.[18] One lawsuit was dismissed and another is pending in Wyoming courts. Women's sororities around the nation are dealing with what should not be a difficult decision: What is a woman, and should men be allowed to live in sorority houses with women? A woman? XX, ovaries, and all—biology's no-brainer. Men in sororities? Nope—those are girls-only zones for sisterhood and safety, not co-ed chaos. America gets it.

Transgenderism and LGBTQ+ rights and demands have dominated the media cycle long enough to spawn a backlash of sorts. One of the poster women for the progressives' diversity juggernaut was Karine Jean-Pierre, President Joe Biden's press secretary. It wasn't enough that Jean-Pierre spoke for the president at White House news conferences, taking and sometimes even answering questions from the media. She also used the White House press secretary's podium as her own bully pulpit, such as to promote her membership in the LGBTQ+ community. During an April 2023 press briefing, she added a personal note emphasizing her key role in the diversity movement, saying, "So this week is Lesbian Visibility Week, and as the first openly queer person to hold the position as press secretary for the president of the United States, I see every day how important visibility and representation are. Today I am honored to welcome the casts of *The L Word* and *The L Word Generation Q*, two Showtime series that chronicle the friendship, the love, the challenges, and the triumphs of strong, funny, and resilient queer women."[19]

I (Carol) once posted this comment on social media: "I feel sorry for this incompetent young lady who makes a mockery of true diversity. Her sexuality is the *only* thing about herself that she seems to value. It's too bad she was placed in such a visible position. Contrived diversity hurts qualified Americans of all groups."

I continue to believe that DEI has harmed the very groups it claimed to protect and advance. In many ways, it demeans highly talented members of the protected groups and throws everyone under a cloud of suspicion, *The Adversity of Diversity* was published shortly after the Supreme Court struck down race-based admissions policies. We correctly argued that that decision would bring about the demise of affirmative action. The details of the case are worth reviewing, referring to *Students for Fair Admissions, Inc. v. President & Fellows of Harvard College* and *Students for Fair Admissions, Inc. v. University of North Carolina*.

Legal experts and higher-education officials on both sides of affirmative action saw the Supreme Court's 2023 ruling against affirmative action coming from miles away, dating back to October 31, 2022. That is when SCOTUS members gathered to hear oral arguments surrounding two similar cases involving similar 2014 lawsuits, one filed against Harvard (a private institution) and the other naming the University of North Carolina (public). The common link between the two cases is an organization known as Students for Fair Admissions (SFFA), which had filed the suits, both claiming that the respective schools' admission policies "discriminated against White and Asian applicants by giving preferences to Black, Hispanic, and Native-American students." In their defense, the two universities claimed their race-conscious admissions policies were necessary to establish and maintain diversity in classrooms, an affirmative action goal considered key to student learning in general.[20]

Edward Blum, creator and president of the plaintiffs' SFFA organization, didn't see the rationale for all the fuss from affirmative action supporters in the months leading up to the Court's ruling. "Ending the consideration of race and ethnicity in college admissions is not a controversial goal," Blum wrote in an email to the *Chronicle*, an independent news organization of Duke University, which itself was following the case closely for its own sake (it was one of seventeen universities that filed an amicus brief on Harvard's behalf, stating it was an invested party). "Those who advocate for the continuation of race in admissions are working against the convictions and preferences of the majority of America's racial minorities," Blum added. In saying this, he also referred to a 2022 Pew Research survey that showed 74 percent of all Americans, including 59 percent of Blacks, 64 percent of Asian Americans, and 68 percent of Hispanics, do not believe race should be a factor in college admissions.[21]

This has not been Blum's first rodeo when it comes to fighting legal battles aimed at overturning race-based college admissions preferences and other comparable types of race-preferential maneuvers. He represented (after having searched for a plaintiff, and found) Abigail Fisher. She was a white student whose application for admission to the University of Texas at Austin (Blum's alma mater) was turned down in the wake of UT's decision in 2003 to abandon its race-neutral admissions policies in favor of adding race and ethnicity to its fifteen admissions criteria. Although the Supreme Court in 2013 upheld the right of UT—and therefore other college institutions—to pursue diversity as a compelling educational interest, in its decision it also put out a stern warning that universities "should first try race-neutral means of achieving diversity before implementing affirmative action," as reported by the *Boston Globe*.[22]

Blum's support of race-neutral policies and practices extends into other fields as well. Soon after he and his wife moved into Houston from the suburbs in 1989, Blum noticed there wasn't a Republican running in his local congressional district's race. When he queried the local Republican Party office to ask why, he was told the district was a majority-minority district and a Republican candidate wouldn't stand a chance. Two years later, Blum ran for the seat and won the Republican primary but later lost to his Democratic opponent in the general election. During his campaign, however, he discovered something that didn't look right. Neighborhoods in his district had been redrawn to bolster minority voting power. This lit a fire in Blum, and he put together a legal team that sued the state of Texas over its allegedly unconstitutional gerrymandering practices—spending eight thousand dollars a month of his own money along the way. Vengeance, to a certain degree, was his. The U.S. Supreme Court found that three of the state's districts were indeed snubbing the Constitution by factoring in race in configuring districts.[23]

So, what does all this about Blum have to do with diversity and diversity training on college campuses and in the corporate world and other workplaces? For one thing, it apparently helped fuel his commitment to end the injustices inherent in reverse discrimination. A word to the wise: Blum apparently isn't finished, and the possibilities are intriguing. Consider what *Boston Globe* reporter Hilary Burns reported in her profile piece on Blum: "Blum has ambitions beyond academia, with litigation in the works to end race-based initiatives in other aspects of American life, including employment diversity programs, corporate board diversity quotas, and government contracting requirements."[24]

Finally, a few words from Blum himself: "The nation cannot remedy past discrimination with new discrimination. There are ways in which individuals and groups who have been on the fringes of opportunity can be brought in, but raising the bar for certain races and lowering the bar for others cannot be the solution to equal opportunity."[25]

Originally scheduled for two hours, the Supreme Court's October 2022 hearings involving the two lawsuits naming Harvard and the University of North Carolina as defendants, reportedly lasted upward of five hours, with the Court's conservative majority spending much of that time grilling affirmative action proponents. Justices Clarence Thomas and Samuel Alito—both among SCOTUS's 6-3 conservative majority—each questioned some of the semantics. "I've heard the word *diversity* quite a few times, and I don't have a clue what it means," said Thomas, an African American. "It seems to mean everything for everyone." Alito said he was baffled by what "underrepresented minority" meant. Fellow Court conservatives Justice Amy Coney Barrett and Chief Justice John Roberts insisted that affirmative action defenders specify an expected end date for when their goals would be met, with attorneys for the universities unable to do so.[26]

The case against Harvard showed that the institution's admissions criteria included a subjective measure of an applicant's traits such as "likability, courage, and kindness, and effectively creating a ceiling for those students [namely, Whites and Asians] in admissions."[27] The subjective "personality test" gave school officials a means to admit lower-qualified students and weed out superior White and Asian applicants without having to defend their admissions policies that were biased against Whites and Asians. Mike and I (Carol) were not surprised by the outcome. We drafted *The Adversity of Diversity* fully expecting the Supreme Court to follow the law and the Constitution. They did!

DIVERSITY RULES

Diversity is at the heart and soul of affirmative action, which explains why diversity, equity, and inclusion (DEI) is closely associated with affirmative action, a connection that does not bode well for DEI programs following the Court's decision to strike down race-based admissions in higher education and the Trump EOs. Whether they know it or not, "companies may be directly impacted by the decision," because of "potential legal challenges to their programs," as stated in a client report released in March 2023 by the Morrison Foerster Law Firm. It noted that "[e]mployers are also increasingly having to navigate the growing trend of state legislation and measures seeking to limit workplace DEI efforts."[28]

It stands to reason that the link between affirmative action and DEI will cause the number of lawsuits challenging the constitutionality of workplace-based diversity programs to proliferate, especially after the Trump EOs. The argument for an historical link between affirmative action and diversity training, or as it is sometimes called "diversity management," appears buttressed by a 1998 paper co-written by Erin Kelly and Frank Dobbin, now college professors. Their premise in "How Affirmative Action Became Diversity Management" is that corporate affirmative action programs actually *became* diversity programs.[29] The question becomes: How did this happen?

To answer this, Kelly and Dobbin argue that Ronald Reagan and his decision after taking office in 1981 to pull back the reins on regulatory oversight and enforcement impacted programs covered by antidiscrimination laws. By 1981, both affirmative action and the Civil Rights Act of 1964 had been in effect more than fifteen years. Many employers had already established diversity programs to manage compliance with the two federal edicts, and they were not about to abandon their efforts because of changes in regulatory oversight. Those efforts had included the establishment of Equal Employment Opportunity (as created by the Civil Rights Act of 1964) and affirmative action offices and activities, which corporations deemed fit and necessary to continue in operation if they were to achieve their affirmative action diversity goals.

Much of the responsibility for diversity training/management's survival, as suggested by the authors of the paper (published in the April 1998 edition of *American Behavioral Scientist*), went to the EEO/AA specialists running the programs. In defense of their work, "they touted the efficiency of formalizing human resources management through such antidiscrimination measures as grievance procedures, formal hiring and promotion systems, and systematic recruitment schemes. Later they invented the discipline of diversity management, arguing that the capacity to manage a diverse workforce well would be the key to business success in the future."[30]

That success in large part remains missing in action. It's time to do something about it, and, in Carol Swain's REAL Unity Training, a proposed alternative solution is presented. We firmly believe diversity without discrimination can be achieved if institutions have the courage and vision to return to a merit-based system that encourages the hiring, retention, and promotion of the best-qualified individuals that apply for positions. It will be necessary for them to abandon the constant bean counting and finger pointing that makes everyone uncomfortable. Diversity done correctly can enhance institutions and lead to more harmonious workplace relationships if employees respect each other's individual talents and contributions. That is more likely to occur when DEI and affirmative action no longer dominate the work environment though the constant barrage of communications about racial, gender, or sexual sensitivity that seem especially designed to spark guilt and shame. Organizations flourish in atmospheres of mutual respect where employees are mission-focused on the needs of the institution. The workplace is not where historic wrongs should be addressed. Instead, employees should focus on the job for which they were hired. Meanwhile, students should be focused on the business of absorbing information and interpreting it using critical thinking skills that have nothing to do with Marxist-based critical theories that focus on indoctrination.

President Trump's EOs takes us back more than sixty years to the original intent and passage of the Civil Rights Act of 1964 which sought to eliminate discrimination based on immutable characteristics. Colleges, universities, corporations, and governmental agencies opened their doors and pursued aggressive outreach and advertising to bring underrepresented racial and ethnic minorities into the system. I (Carol) benefited from these outreach efforts that sought to bring about equal opportunity rather than equal results. In fact, statistics show that the jump in the enrollment numbers of previously underserved minorities started to rise dramatically in the late 1960s. Many prestigious universities in 1969 enrolled more than double the number of black students from a year earlier, a big bump in numbers attributed to the muscle of the whole civil rights movement in league with affirmative action. Columbia University president Leo Bollinger, who had been a first-year law student at Columbia in 1968, remembers the racially based dynamics of that era well. "In that time," Bollinger told the *New York Times*, "there was a sense, pure and simple, that universities had to do their part to help integrate higher education."[31]

HOW AFFIRMATIVE ACTION HELPED RADICALIZE AMERICA

Affirmative action, from its start, was bombarded with complaints, and, surprisingly, the gripes came mostly come from racial and ethnic minorities who felt that they should have been further along. They wanted more positions of power and more opportunities than they had previously held. Many were annoyed that, after decades of purported progress, there still are not enough black and brown faces in certain fields or in certain positions of power; therefore, racism had to be the root cause rather than individual choices and cultural differences that might have impacted the pool of qualified applicants. They believe they are not being well represented in society. Along those lines, we have seen progressive activists such as Derrick Bell, the father of critical race theory, argue that anything Whites do, they do to benefit themselves.[32]

Such dissidents would argue that racism was structural, that it was a systematic entity, not just a collective of random acts of bias or discrimination. That helps explain how and why DEI apparently emerged in tandem with the CRT movement birthed on university campuses, which now reaches into every sphere of American society, including the U.S. military.

Progressives dissatisfied with the pace of progress imposed DEI and CRT on top of affirmative action without much complaint from civil rights advocates who now push for outright discrimination against Whites and Asians. DEI's critical race theory component allows supporters to discount history, facts, and statistical data and anchor their claims on their lived experiences. The lived experiences shared through storytelling, recounting the injustices, outweigh anything a white person has to say about a race-related issue. In other words, an outsider's opinion doesn't count, as in, "How can they possibly know what it's like to be victimized?"

Supporters of affirmative action, and therefore DEI advocates, reject color-blindness; they say it is an impossibility. They do not believe in a meritocracy in which a black man or woman will be fairly and properly rewarded and/or compensated for their work or school performance and achievements. Instead, they believe there should be racial preferences. Not only that, but those preferences should also be only for people who have been discriminated against.

White progressives deny and ignore the accomplishments of millions of successful Blacks from all walks of life who have overcome tremendous odds to make their mark on America. Among those who come to mind are Bob Woodson, Henry Lewis Gates, Ben Carson, Thomas Sowell, William Julius Wilson, and Toni Morrison, as well as historical figures such as Booker T. Washington, W. E. B. Du Bois, and Madam C. J. Walker. There are millions of others who lead and have led successful lives.

In the next chapter, you will learn more about me (Carol) and my story. When I think about my success as a middle-school dropout (ninth grade) who became a highly acclaimed university professor, I think about the opportunities created by the passage of civil rights legislation. By the time I reached college in the late 1970s, affirmative action had a decade of existence under its belt. It was treated as if it were the law of the land instead of the civil rights law signed in 1964. As a high-achieving black woman, I benefited most from encountering people who encouraged me to further my education in an environment where the white people I met wanted me to succeed. Their goodwill and nudges to keep me going occurred in an environment where our national laws prohibited racial discrimination and encouraged institutions and individuals to become talent scouts looking for diamonds in the rough among underrepresented populations. As life would have it, I was the right person at the right time to take advantage of new opportunities in America.

CHAPTER 2

Carol's Educational Journey in an Affirmative Action World

> *"The Congress of the United States has never founded schools for any class of its own people. . . . It has never deemed itself authorized to expend the public money for rent or purchase of homes for the thousands, not to say millions of the white race who are honestly toiling from day to day for their subsistence. A system for the support of indigent persons was never contemplated by the authors of the Constitution; nor can any good reason be advanced why as a permanent establishment it should be funded for one class or color of our people."*[1]

ONCE AGAIN WE HEAR FROM A PRESIDENT JOHNSON speaking during the tumultuous sixties, like how we led off the first chapter of this book. Except this time, it is not LBJ being quoted, but rather Andrew Johnson, the "other" presidential Johnson, who ascended to the U.S. presidency on April 15, 1865, after the assassination of Abraham Lincoln. Andrew Johnson's quote was in reference to the establishment by Congress of the Freedmen's Bureau in the immediate aftermath of the Civil War. It was designed to offer aid to the newly emancipated black slaves. Their newfound freedom was hailed as life-changing, yet it was accompanied by the realization that freed slaves had suddenly been bequeathed the stark reality of starting a new life from scratch, many without a home of their own, a job, or two nickels to rub together.

Andrew Johnson vetoed the Freedmen's Bureau, only for the hostile Republican Congress to override the veto before it nearly succeeded in getting Johnson removed from office.* Johnson's dislike of the proposed Freedmen's Bureau was not born out of racist spite toward black slaves and not wanting to help them in a time of need; it was because the bill ignored poor Whites, many of whom were as destitute as the poorest slaves following the abject death and destruction from the Civil War. In short, Johnson saw the Freedmen's Bureau as a potential source of what almost exactly a hundred years later would become known as "reverse discrimination" as it relates to affirmative action.

Years ago, I (Carol) observed that the first expression of affirmative action, or in this case reparations, came with accusations of reverse discrimination. Newly freed slaves never got their forty acres and a mule, but private philanthropy and government programs have spent trillions of dollars trying to address past and present discrimination against the descendants of slaves. Unfortunately, modern-day affirmative action programs disproportionately benefit the foreign born and those who are affluent. Note that former vice president Kamala Harris, former president Barack Obama, and numerous "black" members of Congress are not descendants of slaves.

In fact, inner-city and poor blacks have *not* been the biggest beneficiaries of affirmative action. Occasionally, some of us slip through the gatekeepers, but for the most part the mobility has not been what one would expect. In 2004, the *Journal of Blacks in Higher Education* reported that in the "late 1960s major universities were recruiting low-income or so-called ghetto blacks. Not so today." Most Blacks at Harvard University and other elite institutions hail from *middle- or high-income families*. The article referenced a 2004 interview in which Professor Henry Louis Gates Jr., then director of the W. E. B. DuBois Institute for African and African-American Research at Harvard, told the *London Observer,* "The black kids who come to Harvard or Yale are middle class. Nobody else gets through." Gates and his colleague, law professor Lani Guinier, noted that two-thirds of the Blacks at Harvard were like Barack Obama and Kamala Harris, in that they were the offspring of immigrants most often from West Africa or the Caribbean.[2]

---

*Andrew Johnson, William J. Clinton, and Donald J. Trump are the only US presidents to be impeached by the US House of Representatives (twice for Trump). None of the men were convicted by the US Senate or removed from office, although Democrats, with the help of an unabashedly compliant left-leaning mainstream media, has gone after Trump nonstop with one flimsy charge after another since he won the election in 2016 and even after he left office in early 2021, their obsession to either get him removed from office (that didn't work) or to derail his 2024 re-election bid.

Carol's Educational Journey in an Affirmative Action World

Affirmative action in some form has been around since I (Carol) was in grade school. When I was in second grade, President Kennedy signed Executive Order 10925 requiring government contractors to "take affirmative action to ensure that applicants are employed, and that employees are treated during employment without regard to their race, creed, color, or national origin." The goal of nondiscrimination was later codified in federal law when Congress passed the Civil Rights Act of 1964 following the longest debate in congressional history. South Carolina Democrat Senator Strom Thurmond's filibuster of the civil rights action lasted twenty-four hours and eighteen minutes, a record that stood until 2025 when New Jersey Senator Cory Booker, a Democrat, spoke for a little over twenty-five hours, mostly doing, what else?, but slamming Trump.

CIVIL RIGHTS MOVEMENT SET THE STAGE

By the time I was born, the civil rights movement was scoring victories that helped set the stage for future success. I was born in 1954, the year that the U.S. Supreme Court issued its ruling in the *Brown v. Board of Education* school desegregation case, but I attended segregated schools until 1968. After completing the eighth grade, I dropped out of school, as all my siblings would eventually do. I married at sixteen and had my first child at seventeen.

I obtained my high school equivalency in 1975. In 1976 I began my academic journey in college, which culminated in an associate degree in business, followed by a bachelor's degree in criminal justice with the distinction of *magna cum laude*, a master's and a PhD (in political science), and a Master of Legal Studies. I wasn't finished. After earning my PhD from the University of North Carolina, I paused my academic studies to take a tenure-tracked position at Princeton University. Then in 1999, circumstances caused me to resume my schooling while taking a sabbatical to earn a Master of Studies from Yale University. After having earned early tenure at Princeton University in 1994, I moved to Nashville in 2000 to teach at Vanderbilt University where I was promoted to full professorship and a joint position in the law school.

Liberals would argue that I used affirmative action to attain success and now I want to pull up the ladder after me. Such an assessment would miss the fact that I worked a full-time job nights and weekends while I was in college and managed to graduate with high honors. Although I was aware of affirmative action, I knew I was smart and I wanted to show that I could compete with the best regardless of race. It was difficult, and sometimes I struggled, particularly with math and science, but I had a strategy, a plan, and a can-do attitude that enabled me to silence the naysayers. Academia was never my idea. White progressives and conservatives recognized my talent and pushed me along a path I never consciously chose.

What benefited me the most was the kindness and benevolence of good people who wanted to see me succeed. They saw potential in me I was unaware of. These people became mentors and encouragers who pushed me far beyond the narrow limits of my imagination. Through it all, I was driven by a desire to prove myself capable. I never wanted to be the weakest link of being an affirmative action hire. Consequently, I refused to apply for the minority positions being offered in political science where job candidates competed within their own groups. I insisted on competing in the general population of applicants and was willing to start at a mid-ranked school and work my way up to Harvard or Princeton. I was persuaded to start my career at Princeton University by an older conservative white man who said, "If you can start at the top, do so. Those other places will always be waiting." Princeton University chose me, and I chose them. I announced when I was hired that I planned to earn early tenure and I did. When I was hired, I had a Harvard University Press contract on my dissertation and I had a National Science Foundation Grant that enabled me to collect data that would turn the dissertation into the prize-winning book *Black Faces, Black Interests: The Representation of African Americans in Congress.*[3]

Black Faces, Black Interests was selected out of 611 titles by *Library Choice Journal* as one of the seven outstanding academic books of 1994, and it won three national prizes. It was the winner of the 1994 Woodrow Wilson prize given to the "best book published in the United States during the prior year on government, politics, or international affairs." It also won the 1995 D. B. Hardeman Prize for the best scholarly work on the U.S. Congress during a biennial period and was a co-winner of the V. O. Key Award for the best book published on Southern politics. *Black Faces* was also cited by Justice Anthony Kennedy in *Johnson v. Degrandy,* 512 U.S. 997, 1027 (1994) and twice by Justice Sandra Day O'Connor in *Georgia v. Ashcroft,* 539 U.S. (2003). Several outside offers of tenure, including one for an endowed chair, soon followed the publication of my book.

I negotiated for early tenure at Princeton, a move I later regretted for how it created animosity among other faculty because the tenure period is normally a seven-year process. By negotiating for early tenure, I was following the examples of white men and women who were highly sought after. I wanted tenure to prove that a person from my background could earn early tenure. My strongest supporters have always been older conservative white men; my greatest opposition has come from progressive Whites who have often joined forces with black liberals to create roadblocks for me.

Academia was never an easy fit for me. Since affirmative action was the dominant focus of institutions, my awards and accomplishments were discounted. In other words, winning the career prize for political scientists did not mean the same thing to the world that it would have meant had I been white. In 2017, while at Vanderbilt, I relinquished my tenure, left academia, and have never looked back. Academia equipped me to do what I do today. I can speak to these issues from a vantage point where I believe I have seen it all. Hopefully, my journey can help others trying to understand and navigate the uncertainty of a world without affirmative action and hopefully without the divisive presence of the DEI purveyors of racism.

DEI: A COTTAGE INDUSTRY

Before diversity, equity, and inclusion became a cottage industry that indiscriminately gave unearned advantages to members of historically marginalized groups, it focused on less-controversial goals of nondiscrimination, outreach, and advertising. Nondiscrimination and the search for talented, hardworking minorities were powerful motivators for institutions. That involved searching for talented members of underrepresented populations and informing them of employment and educational opportunities while publicizing opportunities nationwide to the general population. White men benefited from the advertising of jobs. This helped weaken the word-of-mouth "old boys' network."

If institutions were good at recruitment and honest about their motivations, they were often successful in bringing in people from underrepresented groups and helping them get up to speed. That was the kind of affirmative action from which I benefited as did millions of other people who have been successful in a similar manner since the passage of civil rights legislation in the 1960s. I was a child of that era and a beneficiary of a regime of nondiscriminatory, active recruitment of people from underrepresented populations. I graduated *magna cum laude* while working full time and raising two boys. My Graduate Record Examination (GRE) scores were not outstanding. Also, while in the community college, my lack of a high school background meant that I took remedial courses in math that would later prove crucial to my success in academia. Remedial math helped prepare me for the statistics courses required of social scientists. In fact, my first book and dissertation contained the obligatory regression analyses expected of PhD graduates.

During those years in school, I had an equal opportunity to succeed or fail. Academic leaders and mentors at my schools were looking for bright minorities, so I made sure I was there right in front of them so they could see me. I neither expected nor wanted special treatment. I was able to get admitted to colleges and earn scholarships based on my being an industrious worker who defied stereotypes such as Blacks being inherently unqualified, lazy, or worse.

I benefited from people looking for talented minorities. For me, it was mostly white men who pushed me further than I intended to go; starting out, I was just going to get a two-year degree so I could get a job. I never intended to pursue a PhD, or even become a professor at elite institutions (let alone two such institutions); it was just people I met along the way pushing me because they saw that I was bright. I was able to get attention that a white or Asian student would not have gotten as an honor student. I defied the odds—people knew my name. I profited a lot just from good, old-fashioned common sense and mentorship.

After unsuccessfully applying for jobs as a store manager, I was told I needed a four-year degree. At the same time I also decided I needed to distinguish myself on applications by becoming an honors graduate. Just "make it happen" was my philosophy. That is how I *really* caught people's attention. I checked out library books and purchased others on how to make As in college, how to take essay exams, and how to take objective tests. Then I applied the principles. So, I had a strategy. I knew that if I excelled, it was going to propel me far. Once, when I was struggling in a finite math class at Roanoke College, I dropped the course and, with the professor's permission, I attended the class until the course ended. I took the course for credit the following semester and earned an A.

Many white progressives have been found to hold racist views about the genetic abilities of Blacks. I will never forget when Francis Lawrence, president of Rutgers University in New Brunswick and a staunch supporter of affirmative action, spoke to faculty members about the need to lower expectations for Blacks. In what he thought was an off-the-record conversation, Lawrence stated that Blacks "don't have that genetic, hereditary background to have a higher average" on standardized admissions tests. After his remarks met with calls for his resignation, Lawrence said that he misspoke and didn't really believe what he stated.[4] Surprisingly, he survived the scandal and many high-profile Blacks came to his rescue.[5] Many white progressives, by their actions, indicate they hold the same set of beliefs. That is why they are quick to set up separate graduations, dorms, and class sections for minority students and faculty.

DIFFERENT EXPECTATIONS

White progressives genuinely believe that racial and ethnic minorities are incapable of meeting the same standards as white students. They will not come right out and say that, but their actions speak what their mouths rarely allow to slip out. They also dismiss the minorities who are well qualified and excel in academia and elsewhere. These minorities are the exceptions that prove the rule. The problem now for progressives is that there are not enough of these exceptional underrepresented minorities to satisfy the liberal appetites for proportional representation. So, instead of trying to increase the pool of qualified students, they have been artificially lowering the standards—both to get a desired number of minority students into the school and then to keep them there in good academic standing. Simultaneously, they are getting rid of advanced placement courses, honors courses, and standardized admissions tests. These are among many examples of "affirmative action" in action that make it clear it has been a breeding ground for what we now know as DEI and CRT—outgrowths of affirmative action that play up the victimization angle for Blacks. At the same time they seek to put Whites in their place once and for all, which is in the back of the room, if in the room at all.

It is a similar situation in many high schools. In my home state of Virginia, for example, there were reports in early 2023 of seventeen schools in Fairfax County whose school officials had reportedly failed to notify those students who had achieved National Merit Scholar status. That denied those students the opportunity to tout that recognition on their college applications. It was alleged that school district officials had withheld notice from the award-winning students because they did not want to hurt the feelings of students who fell short of achieving such status. Fairfax County public schools superintendent Dr. Michelle Reid denied the "hurt feelings" allegation, saying the delayed notice for the students was the result of "human error." Reid also disputed a claim made by Virginia

Governor Glenn Youngkin, who, upon hearing the news about the schools, said this was a "maniacal" attempt by the school district to ensure all students receive "equal outcomes."[6] Or what is otherwise known as *equity*.

BLOWING OFF SOME DUST

While writing this chapter, I was performing some light spring cleaning when I opened a drawer and found my senior thesis on affirmative action—the one I referenced earlier—that I had written forty years earlier. That was in 1983 while I was an undergraduate at Roanoke College. I picked it up and read back through its bound pages, all of which had been typed on an old typewriter. I was struck by how well the premise of the paper holds up even today. Remember, too, I was a Democrat at the time, and yet I saw a big problem with affirmative action. Two things really got my attention re-reading my paper: first, how several extended parts of it still resonate and are applicable for present-day discussion, even offering uncanny glimpses of affirmative action's future, and, second, that I got an A+ on it.

Here's an excerpt from that paper that seems as timely today as it was when I was in my twenties:

> Before entering college and the job market, my knowledge of affirmative action stemmed from media accounts. I expected much from the program, considered all Whites opposed to the program racist, and expected my share of the reparations. It took several years of increasingly political awareness and program examination for me to become thoroughly disillusioned with affirmative action. I resent the program that sometimes places incompetent individuals in positions of token authority. Their inevitable foibles are often purposely used to attest to the inadequacies of the program. Furthermore, I resent situations in which competent and sometimes superior minorities are forced to prove that their achievements are earned and not conferred benefits.
>
> Because of these things, I often find myself arguing with white males who say, "You've got it made, you're a black female" or "Why should you study so hard—you've got affirmative action to help you?" The most irritating statement that I've received from these white males was one in which the man lamented, 'I've been looking for a job for two years; if I were a black female, I'd have one.' The average white male seems to believe that minorities are reaping great benefits at his expense. Indeed, he sees us as having food stamps, welfare, practically free education, job preferences, and Medicaid all paid for out of his tax dollars. Moreover, he is quick to point out that he is not responsible for our inferior social

status. He believes that affirmative action is the unjust visiting of the "sins of the father, upon the child."

If nothing else, the fact that there is a 1983 paper of mine that has a timeless feel to it says that I have aged well, too, if I may say so.

A SENSE OF BLACK ENTITLEMENT

The main thing I wanted to show in bringing that paper out of mothballs is how I took such a conservative stance so long ago, when I was still a Democrat. I have always believed that common sense and, as Spike Lee might concur, doing the right thing at any given time and with any given issue, are more important than pledging blind loyalty to a political agenda. In writing about affirmative action, I observed that a lot of Blacks I encountered forty-plus years ago had one of two mindsets: either they believed they were *entitled* to have admissions standards lowered far enough to meet them where they were, or that without affirmative action around to give them a lift they were incapable of success.

Both beliefs were lies. One lie likely prevented students from becoming doctors and lawyers because the academic standards they encountered once they got into a school (thanks to affirmative action) were not as low as they thought they would be—you still must do the work once you get there. If you have a GPA of less than 2.0 and think you are going to be a doctor or lawyer, think again. Not even affirmative action is going to climb that mountain for you. For the Blacks who believed they were incapable of achieving success *without* affirmative action, they were crippled, too.

I have always believed that people are motivated by incentive and will strive to meet any standard standing between them and their life's goal. There was a time when students coming out of high school and wanting to go to elite schools such as Harvard, Yale, Duke, Stanford, etc. thought they knew exactly when they needed to be competitive for admission at elite colleges and universities. Everyone who wanted to go to the Ivy League thought they had to be exceptional. Harvard University, which has never discriminated against Blacks, has always had some among its alumni. Students who wanted to go to a particular school figured out what they had to do to get there. The rules have changed dramatically as DEI has been layered over old-fashioned affirmative action. The quest for equity (*equal results*, not to be confused with *equal opportunity*) stacks the deck against those who played by the old rules. I, for one, do not believe that the elimination of racial preference will yield lily white or Asian institutions; there will always be high-achieving, privileged racial and ethnic minorities who will figure out what they have to do to attain their dream. Bright students will conform their behavior to the environment and the incentive structure placed before them.

Affirmative action stayed around for sixty years until Donald Trump came along with his magical pen. It took enormous courage and vision for him to do what President Reagan decided to let stand. Affirmative action took some legal hits over the years—such as in Michigan. That is where, in 2006, 58 percent of voters approved a ballot initiative banning affirmative action in the state. Not only did the ban affect college admissions, it also put a stop to taking race into account in hiring and contracting. The initiative was challenged the very next day, leading to an eight-year legal fight that moved its way up through courts. Finally, in April 2014, the U.S. Supreme Court ruled that the ban was legal, prohibiting preferential treatment based on race, gender, ethnicity, or national origin.

The Michigan case dates back to 1995. That is when Jennifer Gratz, a young white woman, sued the University of Michigan in Ann Arbor after her application for admission to the prestigious school was rejected. This was despite her 3.8 grade-point average and participation in a variety of extracurricular activities. Gratz, thirty-seven when SCOTUS ruled in favor of the affirmative action ban, predicted at the time that more of the country would follow suit. "I think that this ruling took us one step closer to equality," she said.[7]

I never wanted my two sons to know about affirmative action while they were in high school. I never talked about it around them because I never wanted them to think they could coast because of their race. Affirmative action sends the signal to young minorities that they can be less competent and still get to the same place as their hardworking classmates who happen to be white and end up at lesser institutions. My older son, a factory worker, did not go to college and my younger son became a businessman. For the longest time, my younger son would not apply for work while listing his business as a minority-owned business because he felt it limited his opportunities. Eventually, when he was seeking to subcontract with major firms, he then designated his business as minority owned, as he was advised to do by the corporations wanting to hire his agency. Many corporate and governmental agencies have to solicit bids from a certain number of minority-owned businesses to meet mandated quotas and expectations. The system incentivizes white women and racial and ethnic minorities applying for and taking advantage of whatever programs and funds are available. I have my own businesses as well and have avoided applying for the designation of minority-owned business even though I would have qualified as a Black and as a woman.

THE MISMATCH THEORY

Progressives and well-meaning conservatives who push for lowered college admission standards for racial and ethnic minorities are often doing more harm than good. Back in 2012, Richard Sander and Stuart Taylor Jr., both UCLA law professors, wrote an important book titled *Mismatch: How Affirmative Action Hurts Students It's Intended to Help, and Why Universities Won't Admit It*. Sander and Taylor found that racial preferences often put students at a competitive disadvantage when they found themselves among classmates who were more academically prepared. The affirmative action admittees often found themselves doomed for failure. Eventually, many of the minority students, who could have been successful at a lower-tiered university, never finished. As a consequence, colleges and universities are producing far fewer lawyers, doctors, and engineers than would be expected. Minority law students who manage to graduate fail the bar exam at four times the rate of white students.[8] Of course, Sander and Taylor's study was conducted before DEI's big push for equal outcomes. There has been a move to eliminate tests that disproportionately fail minorities.

We do know that aggressive affirmative action and DEI programs have routinely placed minority students at institutions where many were not prepared to excel. Whenever failure occurs, institutional racism can always be blamed, but not one's level of preparation or intellectual prowess.

When I started college, I began by enrolling at a community college— no affirmative action necessary to attend Virginia Western.

Once I had gotten to Virginia Western and made the dean's list a couple of times, I became receptive to pushing myself to excel. Feedback from prospective employers indicated I needed a four-year degree to become a store manager. I knew from the applications that I needed to distinguish myself if I wanted to get a high-paying job.

My journey took me to Roanoke College, a four-year liberal arts college in Salem, Virginia, then to Virginia Tech, and then to the University of North Carolina at Chapel Hill for my PhD. I would later earn another master's degree in law from Yale University. This was after I had earned tenure at Princeton and before I moved to Nashville to start my full professorship at Vanderbilt. There are minorities (and Whites, sometimes) who are bright and have done well in high school who could do well at the "typical" four-year undergraduate school, but because of affirmative action or sports recruitment, end up instead going to more selective schools where they struggle, and some drop out. If they had gone to a college or university more closely aligned with their academic record, perhaps even a two-year college first, more could have been successful, and some would have graduated at the top of their class rather than in the lower tier. As a GED holder, I needed the community college stint to prepare me for my educational journey. It filled in the gaps and made up for the high school instruction I lacked. My remedial math course prepared me for college math and statistics I would later take at the four-year-college and in graduate school.

I believe my nontraditional path would work for other would-be college or trade school graduates. More strategic choices and planning should be encouraged for young people, and not just for Blacks. It can work for anyone who needs more preparation: the diamond in the rough, for example.

Creative new thinking has come from Harvard University economist Roland Fryer, who happens to be black, like me. In a *New York Times* article titled "Build Feeder Schools (and Make Yale and Harvard Fund Them,)" Fryer noted that the current approach to student recruitment to Ivy League schools is deficient:

"Right now, colleges take the supply of qualified minority students as fixed. They might run a summer enrichment program for local kids, but they don't intervene in students' education in systemic ways. They don't teach the higher-order skills that students need to get into college. They don't cultivate the grit and resilience that kids need to navigate a challenging curriculum after they are admitted. They rely on existing schools to do that—and if those schools routinely fail minority students, well, that's a problem with the precollege pipeline."[9]

Fryer's solution, which is one I wholeheartedly endorse, is for elite institutions to operate and fund feeder middle and high schools for promising students who lack access to a quality education. As far as I am concerned, this approach would be a better use of their vast endowments than the DEI programs and lowered admission standards they fought tooth and nail to retain. To adopt this approach, colleges and universities would have to believe that racial and ethnic minorities are capable of learning and competing with members of the majority group on an equal basis when given the right opportunities.

CHAPTER 3

Diversity Training: A Corporate Conundrum That's Resolving Itself

"Our greatest asset in protecting the homeland and advancing our interests abroad is the talent and diversity of our national security workforce. Under my Administration, we have made important progress toward harnessing the extraordinary range of backgrounds, cultures, perspectives, skills, and experiences of the U.S. population toward keeping our country safe and strong. As the United States becomes more diverse and the challenges we face more complex, we must continue to invest in policies to recruit, retain, and develop the best and brightest from all segments of our population. Research has shown that diverse groups are more effective at problem solving than homogeneous groups, and policies that promote diversity and inclusion will enhance our ability to draw from the broadest possible pool of talent, solve our toughest challenges, maximize employee engagement and innovation, and lead by example by setting a high standard for providing access to opportunity to all segments of our society."[1]

— **President Barack Obama**

THAT IS THE CRUX OF AN OCTOBER 2016 MEMORANDUM titled "Presidential Memorandum—Promoting Diversity and Inclusion in the National Security Workforce." President Barack Obama issued the memorandum less than four months before completing his second term in office. His stern message was directed at the more than three million people who at the time comprised the U.S. national security workforce. That labor pool, according to the memo, entailed the departments, agencies, offices, and other entities found within the "diplomacy, development, defense, intelligence, law enforcement, and homeland security" assets of our federal government.[2]

Obama's eight-page decree encompassed more than twenty-six hundred words and included five major directives outlined in five sections composed of a total of thirteen subsections. A lot to digest there, pushing hard for a PC version of DEI. It offered extensive detail about the procedures and measures these federal departments were to follow and prioritize in focusing their efforts—as prefaced in the memo's titles—specifically in the areas of *diversity* and *inclusion*. The expressed tenor of Obama's directive presumably put diversity and inclusion—you could also include *equity*, albeit unmentioned here, to complete the familiar DEI triumvirate—ahead of other factors such as mission readiness, exclusively merit-based promotions, and quality of training on the pecking order of success criteria for our national security workforce.

Several questions are begged. Was Obama suggesting that solely by increasing the percentage of Blacks and other minorities working in these departments (e.g., defense and homeland security) that their mission readiness would be improved—that more problems would be solved, and with better solutions? And exactly what research was he referring to when he mentioned that "diverse groups are more effective at problem solving than homogeneous groups"? Also, which "homogenous" groups was he referring to (with "homogenous" likely being code for "too white")? He then wrote, "We must continue to invest in policies to recruit, retain, and develop the best and brightest from all segments of our population." Wasn't that already being done?

Obama in his memo called for such geeky-sounding directives as "collection, analysis, and dissemination of workforce data," "aggregate demographic data," "New Inclusion Quotient (New IQ) index score," "barrier analyses related to diversity and inclusion," "voluntary applicant flow data," a requirement that "agencies shall ensure their SES CDP comports with the provisions of 5 C.F.R. part 412, subpart C, including merit staffing and assessment requirements,"[3] and, well, you get the gist. There is nothing like a slew of newly required mind-numbing, time-eating number crunching to further bog down federal government workers while giving America a skewed view of presidential support of the so-called merits of DEI. Notice, too, the timing of Obama's memo—barely a month before the 2016 election, no doubt

Diversity Training: A Corporate Conundrum That's Resolving Itself

so he could show his liberal Democratic base just how genuine his pandering embrace of them was (it didn't work, obviously—Hillary lost). It also sent a late presidential-term shot across the bow of America's corporations, companies, and other organizations, producing a trickle-down effect that served as a warning that they had better get in line with DEI practices as well, or else.

Clearly, DEI, and its forerunner—known simply as diversity and inclusion—had been around decades before Obama fired off his warning-shot memo in October 2016 as part of his farewell tour from the White House. He wasn't breaking new ground on the DEI philosophy and its practice; he was putting his fingerprints on something that stipulated how it would (as opposed to "should") be done. Its roots, as pointed out earlier, date back to the 1960s and the creation of "affirmative action" as introduced in executive orders by JFK and augmented by his successor, LBJ, both of which addressed the workplace as well as college and university admissions offices. What had changed, though, by the time Obama got his boost into the White House, thanks to the political world's version of "affirmative action," is that diversity and inclusion has expanded unchecked into an industry all its own. No longer are DEI programs just an appendage to human resource departments in businesses and on college campuses.

In the last eight to ten years, what we now know as DEI has become a potent and influential cottage industry with a cumulative budget nationwide in the tens of billions of dollars. We now have DEI departments, many led by what's called a chief diversity officer, or something similar, cluttered with untold thousands of DEI professionals whose generous livelihoods are carved out of resources that include taxpayer money as well as dollars that might have otherwise been budgeted for HR departments. As the dominoes have started to fall backward with Trump's EOs and unfavorable court decisions, DEI professionals and their supportive allies in the far-Left ranks are desperately scrambling to validate their continued employment in these roles so they can save as much of that pie as possible for themselves.

DEI PROGRAMS EXPOSED IN
THE ADVERSITY OF DIVERSITY

DEI programs and consultants often use methods that violate the Civil Rights Act of 1964 and the Equal Protection Clause of the Fourteenth Amendment. The Supreme Court decision in the Harvard and University of North Carolina cases shines a spotlight on race-based discrimination and exposes programs for what they really are and what they actually have created in our society. The workplace is rife with political correctness and demands for group privileges that often violate civil rights protections for groups that are not considered historically marginalized. That includes, for example, white males, Christians, and heterosexuals who just want to do their jobs in an environment free of the pressures of social engineering.

Start with their destructive effects on corporate strategy, developing a culture that distracts from profits and market performance, stifling conversation at board meetings that leads to costly nonsensical decisions, stimulating unproductive behavior, and creating a contrarian subculture. Yet DEI advocates and far-Left liberals cling to a false narrative, faithfully parroted by a compliant mainstream media, that diversity, equity, and inclusion remain the key ingredients to success in the corporate world and across all workplace environments. You have those three things in place (or at least believe you do) and the rest is gravy? Probably not. How about market share for your business? Net profits? Year-over-year growth? For many business leaders, those do not seem to matter as much as DEI metrics.

One thing DEI has down cold with all its programs, training, and behavioral edicts is putting white people, especially males, in cages and making them grovel to toe the company line. If you don't embrace the philosophies of aggressive race or gender-based affirmative action, the LGBTQ+ movement, critical race theory, and Black Lives Matter, then it's time to hit the bricks. The same goes with colleges and their DEI mafia with strong-arm tactics of their own, such as if you want an A or B in that history or English class, you had better get in sync with your professor's worldview on gender, race, and American history.

We get it that, legally speaking, the First Amendment and its declaration of free speech applies only to the government's attempted intrusion into our free speech, but you get our drift—the "spirit" of free expression should be voluntarily exercised by all citizens (and their workplace bosses) in all walks of life. It is sad to see how much the far Left insists on trampling on those rights through tactics such as compelled speech in corporations and other organizations insistent on their employees kowtowing/pandering to the politically correct agendas of DEI advocates and activists.

Take it from James Damore, who had been a senior software engineer at Google for four years when in 2017 he got fired for what he described as "perpetuating gender stereotypes."[4] It is not enough that workers—which includes managers and executives—tolerate and are courteous to minority and minority groups (such as LGBTQ) whose lifestyles conflict with a worker's religious beliefs; they also must embrace and endorse such lifestyles, or else. Damore's religious beliefs were not on trial in his case; his rejection of political correctness and right to express his opinions were. His DEI faux pas was a ten-page memo in which he called for the company to back off its obsessive (my word) push for gender diversity in the workplace. Damore's memo zeroed in on Google's diversity and inclusion strategies, among them an unconscious bias class the company was encouraging employees to take, as if they had a choice. He reportedly also argued that gender gaps in the workforce do not necessarily "imply sexism" and that "discriminating just to increase the representation of women in tech" (is) "misguided and biased" (and) "unfair, divisive, and bad for business."[5]

Although Damore was accused of using stereotypical misconceptions about men and women in stating his case, the memo also came out at a time when Google had just updated its internal diversity metrics, apparently admitting that its workforce demographics were skewed heavily male and white. Simultaneous to this, the U.S. Department of Labor had put Google under the microscope amid reports of wage discrimination whereby female employees were allegedly being systematically underpaid. Reaction inside and outside the company over Damore's memo was divided.[6] Some supporters of Damore's right and, in some cases, rationale in writing the memo turned up the heat on Google over the issue of the software engineer's obviously not being allowed to speak freely due to his being fired over the controversial memo.

Google isn't the only high-tech company that has stubbed its toe in the diversity, equity, and inclusion world; Mozilla is another. Mozilla forced the resignation of CEO Brendan Eich in 2014 when it learned that he had made a modest personal contribution of a thousand dollars—*six years earlier*—in support of a gay-marriage ban in California that has since been overturned.[7] When it comes to public and workplace firestorms (especially in California and particularly when it involves a corporate executive supporting a conservative cause), there's nothing so inspiring as going after a company bigwig with a huge public profile when there is no statute of limitations or minimum dollar amount constituting an unacceptable or even unethical political contribution. It is bad for business, apparently, and Eich was toast.

No way Mozilla was going to let this one go (other than Eich being shown the door). As Associated Press reported, "Eich's abrupt departure has stirred the debate over the fairness of forcing out a highly qualified technology executive over his personal views and a single campaign contribution *six years ago*. And it raises questions about how far corporate leaders are allowed to go in expressing their political views."[8] In a DEI world, not very far at all, especially when said corporate leader is white and male, as Eich is. Not just any white male, mind you: Eich not only created JavaScript, but he also had a hand in writing the code for Netscape's Navigator web browser, and he later cofounded Mozilla.[9]

AMERICANS DID NOT SIGN UP FOR THIS

Before you ask, I'll tell you what's wrong with this picture. It is the distasteful type of diversity that is still being pursued by activists today, the one that has been politicized and distorted beyond recognition. This diversity is not the one we signed up for. Diversity's destiny is aimed in the wrong direction. This current version of diversity is not connected to the kind of diversity that we can all pretty much accept and celebrate, the one that we know it when we see it, the one in which everyone can be comfortable that a variety of people are all being given the same opportunity and can blend together without being told how to act. The one in which no single demographic benefits at the expense of another (reverse discrimination). We seek a pure, undefiled brand of diversity absent of legalistic gibberish, rules, and regulations tailored to fit a certain political agenda.

The problem with this altered state of diversity is that those who have been running the diversity, equity, and inclusion industry want people to come into businesses or colleges and universities with group identities. These purveyors of DEI nonsense want to establish affinity groups, then maintain those identities without ever really assimilating (which is foundational to proper diversity), and then to make sure these groups get special protection. They are pushing for proportional representation—actually, *more* than proportional representation. That is, they are not saying that when you get to 14 percent Blacks or 18 percent Hispanics (consistent with the proportional makeup of the general U.S. population), you're done; they want bigger and bigger numbers because they believe the underrepresented are entitled to special treatment. They are pushing and promoting a tact openly hostile to Whites, knowing in this current environment of PC on steroids they will get little pushback, because few opponents dare to try—even when right, they lose.

DIVERSITY TRAINING: A CORPORATE CONUNDRUM THAT'S RESOLVING ITSELF

In my 2002 book *The New White Nationalism in America: Its Challenge to Integration*, I warned that multiculturalism and identity politics, and their attendant language, fostered an environment that would lead to increased racial and ethnic conflict. And it has. The diversity "solution" needs fixing. What is being done now with the likes of DEI and CRT is geared directly and purposely toward creating group conflict that has reached the level of intense tribalism. There is nothing about the DEI approach that seems geared toward bringing people together—no natural blending, integration, or assimilation. It is mostly about conveying the message that it is time for heterosexual white men and women to step aside, that they have had their privileges long enough, and now it is time for members of historically marginalized groups to rule and reign. At the same time, the DEI/CRT movement is sending a message that violence and crime emanating from Black and Hispanic communities is justified because of historical injustices and that antifa members are just freedom fighters who deserve the kid-gloves approach they receive in most cities where they cover their faces like Klansmen and engage in violent behavior against anyone who gets in their path.

Corporate/workplace diversity training (again, what we now call DEI) dates back to the late 1960s and into 1970s. It was a response to the birth of affirmative action and federal legislation that gave us the 1964 Civil Rights Act. Title VII of that landmark Act made it illegal for employers with more than fifteen employees to "discriminate in hiring, termination, promotion, compensation, job training, or any other term, condition, or privilege of employment based on race, color, religion, sex, or national origin."[10] Maybe that explains why those early years of diversity training focused primarily on legislation and compliance (i.e., lawsuit avoidance) in response to a spate of discrimination lawsuits filed with the Equal Employment Opportunity Commission (EEOC).[11]

"Most training during this era was primarily the imparting of knowledge with recitations on the law and company policies, a litany of do's and don'ts and maybe a couple of case studies for the participants to ponder," researchers Rohini Anand and Mary-Frances Winters wrote in "A Retrospective View of Corporate Diversity Training from 1964 to the Present," which was published in 2008. "The length of training varied widely from one hour to a full day, with a typical length of four hours."[12]

DIVERSITY TRAINING: THE EARLY YEARS

In those early years of diversity training, companies and their executive leaders were diligent about compliance, but they were also content to check whatever boxes needed to be checked to mitigate any complaints or lawsuits that otherwise might come their way. Put it another way, they were going through the motions, albeit while playing by the rules of conducting such diversity training. However, rank-and-file employees going through such training (it was usually conducted by HR managers already in place) might remember what they were taught and told, only to forget it days later. Other problems surfaced as well. For instance, because such training at the time focused on underrepresented minorities (think Blacks) and women, those groups' nonmembers—to include white males, of course—felt purposely excluded and came to see such training as preferential treatment of others. As Anand and Winters also point out, the training content itself did not sit well with members of the dominant group (again, white males) because the instruction failed to make much of a connection between recommended changes in behavior among employees and improved business results.

One aspect of the 1960s–1970s diversity training environment that today's social justice warriors can applaud is that industry giants IBM and Xerox jumped into diversity training with both feet. IBM showed its enthusiasm by boldly stating that diversity is a moral imperative, while Xerox put into place an overtly social responsibility tact in creating a diversity training program that went above and beyond what the law called for. No surprise there, though. Rochester, New York—Xerox's home base to this day—had been rocked by riots in the mid-sixties and in 1971 was hit with a class action discrimination suit.[13]

Some fifty years later, diversity/DEI training had morphed into something almost unrecognizable to what C-level and HR executives were dealing with in the Aquarius days of yesteryear. In case you have not noticed it, this whole DEI/CRT/BLM and even LGBTQ+ alphabet-soup programming—with their seething watchdog influence over corporate America and workplace diversity training in general—is all part of the American version of Marxism. I have seen presentations of these agendas; critical race theory comes straight out of Marxism. That's not us stretching things to the nth degree to make a connection; by their very nature and definition, CRT, critical queer theory, and so forth are subcategories of Marxism. If you are a far-Left progressive and either do not know that or deny that connection, then you have not done your required reading of the Marxist playbook—it is the overarching umbrella. You need to do your own homework; it's your philosophy we are talking about here, after all. At the end of the day (and morning, afternoon, and night for that matter), Marxism in its radical nature is all about upending society. It is not about bringing people together, or racial healing, or reconciliation, or bringing about any type of unity into America. It is all about division.

THE BLACK LIVES MATTER FACTOR

As much as BLM has been a ringleader—you, too, LGBTQ+—in this "progressive" crusade to hold corporations hostage to their whims, and as much as BLM has gotten into the heads of the likes of National Football League Commissioner Roger Goodell, it's interesting to note that as of June 2023, as we were writing *The Adversity of Diversity*, BLM was apparently already on life support, teetering on the edge of bankruptcy.[14] Chalk that up to the reported failures of individual leadership that has allegedly pocketed millions of dollars in wealth/real estate holdings for themselves, much of it eagerly donated by corporations such as Warner Bros., looking to promote their "antiracist" agenda, all the time making no secret of their ties to Marxism.

Yes, BLM's questionable business dealings and accounting practices have earned the race-driven organization a spot in this discussion about diversity training. How so? It's how the likes of Warner Bros. had signaled their antiracist virtues[15] by sending big bucks to BLM, which apparently makes up for any deficiencies they might have in their own in-house DEI training programs. Law professor and legal scholar/commentator Jonathan Turley put it thusly: "(BLM co-founder Patrisse Marie Khan-Cullors) was previously open about her lack of interest in working with 'capitalist' elements. Nevertheless, BLM was run like a Trotskyite study group as the media and corporations poured in support and revenue. It was glaringly ironic to see companies like Warner Bros. falling over each other to grab their own front person as the group continued boycotts of white-owned businesses. Indeed, if you did not want to be on the wrong end of one of those boycotts, you needed to get Cullors on your payroll."[16] And what a payoff it was for Cullors and others in charge at BLM. Tens of millions of contributed dollars (or what Don Corleone might call "protection money") flowed into their coffers at Black Lives Matter Global Network Foundation, more than $6 million of which went to Cullors and other Canadian activists for the 2021 purchase of a Toronto mansion.[17]

Until the Trump EOs were signed, when I (Carol) saw a white male child, I saw someone who was going to have a lot of problems down the road because of his skin color. The tables had seemingly been turned against Whites. Trump's EOs make it far more likely that nonminorities will get a fair shot at equal opportunity in the workplace and college admissions. Their skin color is no longer baked into the system as a factor that places them at a disadvantage. A strong commitment to nondiscrimination and equal opportunity will help create a more just system where no one is advantaged or disadvantaged because of their skin color.

When I (Carol) have given presentations to homeschooling families, I have emphasized the need for parents and students to know the truth about DEI and CRT; otherwise, when their kids finish their education and enter colleges and universities or the work world, they will risk being blindsided by what they will certainly encounter. White males will still encounter prejudicial information telling them that their race is responsible for the injustices around the world and that they bear guilt for the unfortunate situation many racial and ethnic minorities experience. Hopefully, there will be less of the shaming and indoctrination going forward. In the past, CRT/DEI-related bullying and shaming on college campuses traditionally began when the student began to receive literature from the institution. Orientation week was like drinking water from a firehose for many students raised in traditional Christian families. Students would then be in for a massive cultural shock when they encountered the world of work and life on the modern campuses. It did not matter much whether the institution was Christian or secular. The playbook was usually the same everywhere.

Life after race-based affirmative action has clear implications down the road for the DEI officers and trainings that have engulfed every sector of our society, including the U.S. military. That's where Trump's secretary of defense, Pete Hegseth, has worked diligently to return the armed forces to a meritocracy. Nevertheless, medical schools and the aviation industry have made diversity hiring decisions that will impact safety until institutions can gradually bring back an emphasis on merit.

This is what life in a post-DEI/affirmative action world demands. We need substantive conversations about the diversity that can emerge naturally from a merit-based system that complies with the law and utilizes objective criteria for hiring and firing. Institutions need to examine themselves and have honest discussions about the qualifications of the people hired, the teams they form, and how these strengthen the mission of the organization.

We know from the higher education examples that led to the end of affirmative action that all the courses, protests, DEI deans, and cultural engagement employees failed to advance racial healing or reconciliation. Instead, they have encouraged segregation and resegregation with their separate dorms, separate class sections, separate this, and separate that. *That* has been divisive. People in the corporate world learned that many of their young executives educated under that DEI system took their values into their corporate world often to the detriment of the company. It became a corporate problem, affecting C-level executives on down. Instead of being able to focus on true success-or-failure criteria, such as profit margins, year-over-year growth, market share, and adherence to the mission of the founders and owners, they were forced to babysit, nurse, and put out fires and lawsuits related to DEI done the wrong way.

Things are changing for the better. Our hope is that readers will see that the elimination of affirmative action and DEI is positive. It does not mean a return to male-dominated, lily-white organizations and institutions.

CHAPTER 4

A Not-So-Inconvenient Death: The Martyrdom of George Floyd

"Never allow a good crisis to go to waste. It's an opportunity to do the things you once thought were impossible."[1]
— **Rahm Emanuel**, White House Chief of Staff under President Barack Obama, 2009-2010, writing for the *Washington Post*, March 25, 2020

"The murder of George Floyd on May 25, 2020, unleashed a tidal wave of pledges of support for greater diversity, equity, and inclusion (DEI) across corporate America and beyond. Companies scrambled to voice their support for Black Lives Matter; they created and filled new positions for chief diversity officers, and announced their commitment to increasing their efforts to hire and retain more people from underrepresented, underprivileged, underappreciated segments of the population."[2]
— **Paolo Gaudiano**, writing for *Forbes*, June 27, 2022

THE FIRST PART: HORRIBLE NEWS, PARTICULARLY FOR THOSE PEOPLE who knew and loved George Floyd, but good news for the DEI industry. It finally had found its best rallying opportunity in years.

Rahm Emanuel was right.

Emanuel, a former Illinois congressman and eventually a mayor of Chicago after leaving his White House post less than two years after being appointed to it by President Obama, has never run from his controversial quote (on loan from the archives of noted political theorist and radical activist Saul Alinsky). In fact, Emanuel wrote about seeing the brighter side of a national crisis or tragedy in his March 25, 2020, editorial in the *Washington Post*. This was days after the U.S. started shutting down in the wake of the arrival of the COVID-19 crisis, and exactly two months ahead of Floyd's death attributed to the hands (or bent knee) of a white cop in Minneapolis.[3]

Worth noting, giving the historical significance of Floyd's death, is the initial autopsy report by the Hennepin County Medical Examiner's Office. It described Floyd as having COVID with the cause of death listed as a "cardiopulmonary arrest complicating law enforcement subdual, restraint, and neck compression." Fentanyl and methamphetamine were in his bloodstream and he suffered from heart disease and hypertension. Independent medical examiners hired by the family concluded that the death was homicide with one of the expert witnesses describing him as being in good health.[4]

To bring perspective to Emanuel's quote above, it helps to know that he at one time was tagged as a "bulldog" or "attack dog," dating back to his days as an aide in the Bill Clinton administration. Referring to the spreading pandemic in that *Post* article, Emanuel said that then-President Donald Trump was "outmatched by the moment," and, furthermore, immediate mobilization was needed "to think strategically not only about how to address the virus but also about how the United States can come out stronger on the other side."[5] On this side, however, thousands of Americans a week were already dying from a rampant global virus. Opportunities during tragic times like this can only arise in the eyes of sociopathic beholders—such as BLM, antifa members, and other racially divisive activists.

Emanuel's seemingly ruthless words could be interpreted as even more fitting in the aftermath of the death of Floyd, a black man who, while on the ground and in police custody, succumbed as Minneapolis cop Derek Chauvin kept him pinned to the ground with a knee.[6] As news of the manner of Floyd's death flashed across America, anti-White activists went to work as if on cue. The death of Floyd, a black man, at the hands of a white cop was their green light, a chance to seek "social justice" by wreaking havoc nationwide through violence, protests, and destructive acts such as burning businesses. People died. It wasn't long before local government officials and angry citizens started calling for the defunding—some even mentioned "disbanding"—of police departments, as rioting and related violent crime spiked in many areas.

A Not-So-Inconvenient Death: The Martyrdom of George Floyd

This all had the appearance of mass insanity, except it wasn't. If you look closely in the right places, you will see that these waves of protests, violence, and destruction, to include the burning of businesses, were part of the radical progressive playbook, to include the parts about being orchestrated and well-funded. There was nothing random or authentic about any of it. All it takes to put the master plan in motion is a spark that lights the fuse, and Floyd's death was that spark. The fact that the perpetrator was a white cop was a bonus. It was too good a crisis to pass up. It screamed *opportunity*. Alinsky and Rahm were right. And Floyd? He was as much a useful patsy as he was a mourned martyr.

CORPORATE AMERICA TOLD TO JUMP, BUT HOW HIGH?

Much of corporate America immediately went into overdrive launching their own crisis responses, and they knew what needed to be done to save or preserve face: just as Gaudiano described above, underneath the Emanuel quote. Many companies, perhaps sensing they were about to be pressured or even bullied at the end of a proverbial bayonet, pledged to beef up and push harder than ever before with their DEI programs and practices, all in the spirit of workplace affirmative action guidelines. It was also to make a public showing of their enhanced efforts to fight racism in their communities. If BLM leaders had asked (told) corporate executives and board members to jump, they likely would have responded, "How high?" What choice did they have?

Here's a choice, as reported in the *New York Post* on July 10, 2020. Within weeks of Floyd's death, the city of Seattle's Office of Civil Rights sent out an email invitation asking, "white city employees" to be present for a training session titled "Interrupting Internalized Racial Superiority and Whiteness," a presentation intended to help white employees examine their "complicity in . . . white supremacy" and "interrupt racism, in ways that are accountable to black, indigenous, and people of color." It was also reported that Seattle's trainers explained to seminar attendees that "white people have internalized a sense of racial superiority, which has made them unable to access their 'humanity' and caused 'harm and violence' to minorities."[7]

Christopher F. Rufo, author of that *New York Post* piece, noted in his story that James Lindsay, also a noted critic of DEI training, had opined that the content of that training session, as described here, wasn't "the language of human resources; it is the language of cult programming—persuading members that they are defective in some predefined manner, exploiting their vulnerabilities and isolating them from previous relationships."[8]

DEI training? How about we instead call it what it really is: BCW Training—Boot Camp for Whites? Seattle in recent decades has painted itself as a champion of the political correctness movement to include standing guard as a true DEI trooper, a lightning rod for diversity and diversity training notoriety. Which brings us to Seattle-based Starbucks. You might remember hearing about the April 2018 incident at a Starbucks facility in the Philadelphia area. That was the one in which two black men who had entered the Starbucks were asked to leave after they had been spotted by Starbucks employees sitting at a table for quite a while without ordering anything. The two men, who declined to leave when asked by management, claimed they were waiting for a business associate. That meeting never took place, however, because the two men eventually were led out of the facility in handcuffs by police who had been called by a store manager.[9]

Enter Shannon Phillips, a regional Starbucks manager in the Philly area. She was fired after having defended a white restaurant employee who, in turn, had been put on administrative leave for alleged discriminatory conduct. For sticking up for the employee put on leave, Phillips herself was fired. About a year later, Phillips filed a lawsuit saying, by her being fired, she had been discriminated against because of her race. A classic case of reverse discrimination. No White privilege there. Four years later, though, in June 2023, a New Jersey jury returned a verdict of $25.6 million in favor of Phillips. That included $25 million for punitive damages and $600,000 in compensatory damages, according to the law firm that represented Phillips.[10] Soon after the original incident, Starbucks closed about 8,000 of its stores for an afternoon of mandatory anti-bias training for 175,000 of its employees. Looney Tunes stuff like this is going on all around America, masquerading as diversity/DEI training and being forced down the throats of workers who have no option but to listen to this nonsense and try to swallow it (or not).

Wokeness has its cost. By July 2022, Starbucks was in the news again because of its decision to close sixteen stores in urban areas (five of those in Seattle) because of crime and rampant drug use. Backtracking on its free public use of bathrooms, Starbucks store managers now have the discretion about when to hand out the key. Keyed bathrooms have now become the norm even in cities as far flung as Nashville.[11]

A Not-So-Inconvenient Death: The Martyrdom of George Floyd

A STICKY SITUATION

Granted, the Floyd aftermath simultaneous to the COVID outbreak was a sticky time to be a company executive or business owner. Corporate America was already reeling from having to wrestle with panicky local, state, and federal authorities issuing mandates and protocols regarding which businesses were deemed essential and which were not. Not to mention how to handle such issues as masks, social distancing, and, eventually, vaccine distribution and administration amid misinformation and false narratives relative to proper health care of apparent COVID patients.

The elephant in the room: what to do about diversity, equity, and inclusion (DEI) programs in workplaces now that it was time once and for all to put white people—especially *white males*—and most especially *conservative white males*—in their rightful place and to stamp out so-called White privilege and White supremacy. DEI advocates, managers, and trainers were handed a renewed and enhanced level of clout they had never had before; meanwhile, Marxist-influenced progressives were rubbing their hands in gleeful anticipation of what they could get away with next. Floyd's death had essentially weaponized DEI practices and training against Whites—not a chance of a two-way street here.

History was repeating itself from more than fifty years earlier. Just two or three years after the Civil Rights Act of 1964 was signed into law, America witnessed its worst race riots ever. At the time, in the late sixties, affirmative action, racial preferences, and what was then simply called *diversity training* (all things most Americans say they no longer want or need) were designed to appease would-be rioters. So much for that. For decades, the Left has used a strategy of violence and protests to get what they want. It's their nature. They create a narrative out of thin air that may or may not be true, but repeat it enough times prominently—with the help of much of the media—that anyone content like sheep to buy into the liberal malarkey accepts the liberal narrative as gospel *truth*. It was *not* the down-and-out people who were rioting now, it was the elites. Alinsky would have been proud if he had still been alive to see this. Rahm likely was nodding his head as if to say, "See, I told you this stuff works. If you build it (a crisis), they (opportunists) will come."

Since the Floyd debacle, the dial on the divisiveness quotient of DEI training had been cranked up to high; it was in the red of the danger zone. This first started becoming evident while Barack Obama was in the White

House. No coincidence there. Under him, DEI became more aggressive. At the time, I was still a university law professor and aware of what was happening at colleges and universities. Because of trickle-down orders and mandates from the Obama administration, prospective employees and students were forced to take certain oaths or write and sign statements declaring their support for various forms of diversity. This now included far-Left agendas espousing LGBTQ+ principles, even when those ran counter to a prospective employee's or student's faith/religious beliefs. That is known as compelled speech, or compelled acts, and goes against the grain of the U.S. Constitution as well as Christian morals and ethics. Tolerating homosexuality, queerness, or transsexualism is one thing; being forced to embrace, promote, or endorse those lifestyles is another—it's likely in violation of free speech as stated in the First Amendment. Marxist progressives have been empowered and emboldened to shove those types of shenanigans upon applicants, apparently nonchalant to the possibility that courts could rule them as sexual harassment.

While we were working on *The Adversity of Diversity*, the Texas senate passed a bill that would prohibit universities from forcing applicants to swear such oaths or sign such statements. It was signed into law, making Texas the second state (Florida was the first) to ban DEI programs at public universities. Such programs should be prohibited at every college and university in the nation because they are based on practices and approaches that violate the rights of nonfavored groups. A number of Women's Studies programs have for decades been requiring job applicants to express support for LGBTQ+ lifestyles. At some of the more elite institutions, it is a given that new directors of such programs must be either a member of the LGBTQ+ community or someone with a track record that can easily demonstrate their commitment by writing or signing a statement swearing to such.

One distinction needs to be pointed out here. Leftist advocates for diversity training and similar programs keep insisting that DEI, affirmative action, and the teaching of CRT were three separate entities that had to be treated distinctively from one another—that, for example, DEI and affirmative action are not the same (they are, in fact, essentially the same). Leftists have long said they are different so that if the Supreme Court were to strike down or at least considerably weaken affirmative action (which it did, ultimately), DEI would be less likely to be affected. Therefore it could continue unscathed as the $50 billion industry it is, still employing tens of thousands, all with expectations of continued job security. Well, not so fast, obviously.

In its original form, in the late sixties, diversity training was. in fact ... drum roll ... diversity training. As it should be. That is no longer the case. *Diversity training morphed into something more resembling divisiveness training.* I'd even go so far as to say it became divisiveness indoctrination, a form of social re-engineering. The Left's aim is for it to be a mechanism that promotes social justice.

If your workplace scheduled one of those special days where everyone had to, say, wear a purple ribbon to virtually signal their approval, support, or endorsement of a certain cause or movement, and you either refused to wear the purple ribbon or choose to stay in your office all day while not taking it off, you risked punishment if what you were deemed as rejecting that day's mandated cause or engaging in borderline insubordination.

As of 2023, instances of reverse discrimination were continuing to dot the American landscape. Another notable example involved the University of Minnesota, which faced backlash in 2023 after its Office of Undergraduate Studies launched a taxpayer-funded summer research program that was made available only to nonwhite students. In fact, it was a paid undergraduate internship program (each student selected for the program received a $6,000 stipend) in which applicants were required to submit demographic information about themselves.[12] The institution is currently among the colleges being investigated for race-based discrimination.[13]

Where's the fairness in that? Not much diversity being practiced there.

"There is no good form of racial discrimination," Bill Jacobson, president of the Equal Protection Project said, referring to the University of Minnesota case. "It's shocking that a major university would so openly make educational opportunities open only to students of a certain skin color. . . . U. Minnesota's conduct is inexcusable."[14]

College campuses are ripe for (and rife with) a variety of diversity-related issues. One credo in all this: Be careful what you say or write, as I found out the hard way concerning a newspaper column I wrote some years back, critical of and questioning certain tenets of Islam related to violence. I first experienced it at that time when I was still a college professor and wrote the opinion piece criticizing Islam. Apparently offended by what I wrote (that is what is now known as a *microaggression*), a hipster-identifying student from California wrote to all my website advertisers telling them that if they didn't stop advertising with me, he was going to organize a boycott of their businesses. A couple of them quietly ended their advertising for me with only the staunchest conservatives being undeterred by the threats.

For many people, this has become the American way of doing business. That could be construed as blackmail or extortion, unless you are an underrepresented class of people, i.e., "minorities." Some groups have stepped up their aggressive, intrusive attacks against conservatives or corporations that don't give them special treatment.

Case in point is LGBTQ+, a far-Left cause which has become powerful and even ruthless in how they target businesses. The message: you'd better play ball with them, and they get to make all the rules. That is going on all over the country, and it's no longer just about getting a fair shake, equal rights in the workplace, and respect in the court of public opinion; it's about forcing onto us their views, beliefs, and lifestyle and gender-related choices—some of them of highly questionable moral character, such as drag queens instructing and even touching children at public events. Recall how, during Pride Month in June 2023, LGBTQ+ (lesbian, gay, bisexual, transgender, queer, etc.) groups and activists were celebrated nationwide the entire month, such as in pregame events at Major League Baseball ballparks. Some of the displays were overtly distasteful and of a crude sexually suggestive nature, all the while getting gobs of favorable national attention from hordes of media apparently eager to help promote the cause.

Because LGBTQ+ influence and activities have likely been riding the coattails of George Floyd's martyrdom and the aftermath of his death, corporations and other businesses across America have been put on notice that gender- and sexuality-identification issues in the workplace require immediate attention and remedial action. In an upside-down world where transactress and influencer Dylan Mulvaney (who transitioned from male to female in 2021) has become a national icon representing and promoting brands such as Nike, Anheuser-Busch, and Kate Spade, much of corporate America has hustled to climb aboard that bandwagon to protect the viability of their own names and brands. The incentive that has whipped them into shape? A scoring system known as CEI, which stands for corporate equality index, managed by the Human Rights Campaign (HRC), reportedly the largest LGBTQ+ political lobbying group in the world.[15]

Funded in part by millions of dollars donated by George Soros's Open

Society Foundation, as well as other entities' contributions, according to the *New York Post*[16], HRC issues report cards that keep the U.S.'s biggest corporations "in line" by grading them on a 100-point scale, measuring how well they implement certain criteria: workforce protections (no employment discrimination based on sexual orientation of gender identity); inclusive benefits (such as providing health care for same-sex couples); supporting an inclusive culture (i.e., trans-inclusive restroom/facilities policy); corporate social responsibility (marketing to LGBTQ+ consumers, for example); and responsible citizenship (you lose points for donating to organizations that advocate against LGBTQ+ equality). James Lindsay, a prominent political commentator and anti-DEI proponent, describes the HRC's administration of the CEI to be "like an extortion racket, like the Mafia."[17]

SOMETHING CALLED THE 'CORPORATE EQUALITY INDEX (CEI)'

CEI is part of a larger, growing entity known as ESG (Environmental, Social, and Corporate Governance), which has been described as an "ethical investing" operation "increasingly promoted" by the nation's three biggest investment firms—Blackrock, Vanguard, and State Street Bank. ESG funds are invested in companies that obediently oppose fossil fuels, favor unionization, and place a higher priority on racial and gender equity than they do merit-based hiring and board selection.[18]

According to the *New York Post*, this triumvirate of firms is among the top shareholders of most U.S. publicly traded companies. That puts them and their ESG orthodoxy in position to wield considerable control over many of the top corporate management teams and boards, "and they determine in many cases executive compensation and bonuses and who gets re-elected or reappointed to boards," says entrepreneur and *Woke Inc.* author Vivek Ramaswamy, who was a Republican candidate for president in 2024. "They can make it very difficult for you if you don't abide by their agendas."[19]

Going against LGBTQ+ training in your workplace can be hazardous to your career's health. Raymond Zdunski, a western New York account clerk for a public organization that provides education materials to school districts in the state, was fired in 2018 for refusing to attend mandatory LGBTQ+ training. He sued, stating that the scheduled training sought to change "his religious beliefs about gender and sexuality . . . and would have caused him to violate the religious teachings to which he adheres." About four years later,

51

a district court judge dismissed the lawsuit, claiming that Zdunski's claims were unsupported. The 2nd U.S. District Court of Appeals upheld the lower court judge's ruling, saying Zdunski had failed to provide "sufficient evidence" backing up his claims.[20]

The Left and its constituent companies, organizations, and associations were effective at intimidating conservative businesses, using pressure tactics that interfere with not just freedom of speech but also the freedom of commerce. It was "their time" and it was open season on Whites and conservatives, in particular—Asians, too, to some degree, at least in educational circles. The pendulum swung in favor of the Left and DEI programs in the three years after Floyd's death. It has now started to swing back in the other direction. Before this recent shift, Whites and conservatives had been victims of old-time holdups, just like in the old Westerns with the shoot-'em-up bad guys robbing a train.

The ramped-up DEI intrusion that followed Floyd's death was described as an "ideological creep." That was the phrase the *Epoch Times* used in a headline over an article in which it was reported that the "DEI industry (was) on a mission creep, and while anti-DEI measures (were) curtailing woke brainwashing in some workplaces, DEI promoters (were) busy insinuating it into others." Such as making DEI training a required element of continuing education for practicing lawyers, with eleven states now making it mandatory for attorneys to accrue "diversity and inclusion" course credit hours to keep their law-practice licenses.[21]

It was a similar story in the healthcare field. In 2022 the Association of American Medical Colleges published its official DEI competencies to be adapted into curriculum development for medical schools, post-graduate residency programs, and faculty training. Those competencies reportedly include one that describes "the impact of various system of oppression on health and healthcare (e.g., colonization, White supremacy, acculturation, assimilation)."[22]

Much of the mainstream media remained faithful to the enhanced "wokeness" of the DEI industry, consistently giving glowing reports of "how well" DEI training has done in addressing such problems as White privilege and White supremacy, and supposedly making our country—at least our workplaces—much safer and more cognizant of the value of social justice and DEI's positive effect on the world.

A Not-So-Inconvenient Death: The Martyrdom of George Floyd

A GAME CHANGER FOR CEI?

As of March 23, 2025, a handful of bold companies are confidently stepping back from the Corporate Equality Index (CEI). They've got a cheerleader in Robby Starbuck, a savvy activist shaking up the corporate world. Big names such as Ford, Tractor Supply Co., and Harley-Davidson—there are seven in total—saw their 2023-2024 CEI scores dip by 25 points after smartly rethinking DEI commitments, a move sparked by Starbuck's push against what he calls "woke" overreach.[23] Tractor Supply Co. even waved goodbye to HRC data submissions entirely in 2024, while Target dialed back after a 2023 boycott lesson. This is proof these firms are tuning into a shifting vibe, with a 31 percent drop in CEI chatter in earnings calls signaling a fresh, pragmatic focus.[24]

Robby Starbuck's X-fueled crusade is the real game-changer here. He is inspiring companies to ditch what he celebrates as unnecessary fluff for a "common sense" win that's got people talking and companies shifting away from DEI.[25] Nevertheless, the 2025 CEI still has 1,449 participants—765 nailing perfect scores,[26] but Starbuck's influence is a lifeline for companies that want to get back to the business of business.

GOODBYE TO 'EQUALITY'; HELLO TO 'EQUITY'

On the one-year anniversary of George Floyd's death, CNBC reported on corporate America's progress in terms of reforming their workplace practices to fight against and reduce racism. CNBC asked a half-dozen business executives, activists, and thought leaders involved in this reform what progress they had seen in the previous twelve months. Walmart President/CEO Doug McMillon mentioned, ". . . we've seen the private sector step up in response to racial injustice and inequity . . . " Maxine Williams, Facebook Chief Diversity Officer: ". . . companies are becoming more bold in acknowledging inequities . . ." Carlos Cubia, Global Chief Diversity Officer at Walgreens Boots Alliance: "The racial equity movement opened not only eyes, but minds." Then there is this, from Connie E. Evans, President and CEO of Association for Enterprise Opportunity: "There must be a long-term approach to promoting equity for black and brown business owners . . . " and, "Companies will also fall short if they have not made internal changes to address equity . . . "[27]

Consider what each of those comments had in common. The use of the word *equity* in one form or another, a word which many people believe to be synonymous with *equality*, when in fact it is not. Progressives slyly sneaked *equity* into many conversations about race, diversity, inclusion, and affirmative action. Equity, in this context, means that, as a member of an underrepresented group, you will not only be given a boost in the hiring process (diversity) and an inside track for positions of added influence (inclusion), your performance metrics on the job will receive a favorable grade, score, or rating higher than your actual performance should have earned. It's much like being graded "on the curve" during exam time in school.

I (Carol) know of numerous business owners who have developed and cultivated highly successful workplaces with motivated employees representing healthy mixes of races, beliefs, and backgrounds by implementing and promoting unifying business practices that build morale and lift bottom lines. Some of the things these innovative entrepreneurs and companies have in common are commitments to caring for employees and encouraging them to care for themselves; inspiring ideas, creativity, and clear, open communication; active listening with consistency and empathy; ensuring leadership fully understands the organization's mission and vision, and can clearly articulate and model it to others; and embracing and celebrating diversity according to biblical principles, which by their very nature are inclusive, as well as other virtuous practices.

Those precepts and guidelines might sound radical to many people, and that is a shame because they are all rooted in what we know to be traditional, foundational values easily understood and appreciated by people from a variety of backgrounds. Put it this way: Which of those practices and precepts would you consider to be poisonous to the workplace in terms of divisiveness? None, right? It shouldn't take a presidential executive order or an act of Congress to make mandatory what needs to be done. We have lost our way.

"If profit is a part of any business, then social responsibility should be its soul," we were told by Rebecca Weber, chief executive officer of Association of Mature American Citizens (AMAC), a U.S.-based conservative advocacy organization and interest group with more than two million members. (Note: Weber is among about a dozen corporate human resources executives/managers interviewed for general background information used in this book.) "We feel a responsibility to take care of our associates. Their health needs and their families will always come first, before the demands of business. We demonstrate that through our flexibility. We have the right people and they don't take advantage or abuse it.

"Our work comes and goes, but at the end of our lives we don't really remember the business deals but we do remember our loved ones. We encourage building those memories. Our mission is focused on faith, family, and freedom, and we apply that to the way in which we manage people. We allow people to take off for different faith holidays they celebrate. We don't want to lose sight of what is most important—health and families."

Most American companies stuck and reliant on DEI programs have gone about it all wrong: pursuing, chasing, and conducting what evolved into a common type of in-house business strategy rooted in affinity groups, suspicion, intolerance, workplace bias, reverse discrimination, divisiveness, and, ultimately, self-destruction. In fact, those factors are what led to a backlash against the DEI industry, pushing it toward irrelevance and eventual obsolescence in a world where affirmative action had long outlived its constructive purpose. In the places where it still exists, DEI continues to miss the mark on how to heal this country, both in the workplace and extending into the home. Companies that now cling to DEI and affirmative action risk costly lawsuits. Nondiscrimination is one path forward for diversity without discrimination.

There is a better way to achieve diversity goals, and we will soon get to more details of what REAL Unity Training should look and feel like as a worthy replacement for failed DEI training.

CHAPTER 5

DEI Training and Its Descent into Divisiveness

"The idea of diversity is that you're bringing people with different perspectives together in order to create something that is a more profitable or productive whole. When you have functional diversity, it actually does seem to produce results. It does seem to actually help you overcome bigotry if that's a thing that is still a problem for you. But there are ways that work, and there are ways that don't. . . . For example, putting people in mixed groups and having them work toward a common goal, they tend to forget about the differences and work toward the common goal, and to bond in the process. This is actually something that is well-known and has evidence. . . .

"I don't want to give this idea that diversity means communism. I want to make the argument that diversity is a very colonized tool that has been purposed, and the reason that diversity has been so interesting . . . is because there were some big open doors created for it by the Supreme Court primarily that opened the door to gigantic industries for diversity trainers, whose manuals started coming out in the seventies. Now, people like Robin DiAngelo [American author of such titles as White Fragility, Nice Racism, and Seeing Whiteness] write these manuals and make obscene money.

"There is a difference between how normal people would view diversity—some functional goal is being achieved by bringing people with different perspectives together—vs. how the woke are going to see diversity, which is

going to be in terms of that the only relative thing is power dynamics in terms of creating difference. [For them it comes down] to identity politics."[1]
— **James A. Lindsay,** American author and cultural critic, excerpted from a segment of his April 2023 New Discourses video presentation, entitled "The Marxist Roots of DEI Workshop: Session 2—Diversity." This excerpt was edited for clarity and length.

DIVERSITY, EQUITY, AND INCLUSION (DEI) IS SHORTHAND for the present-day mantra of the type of workplace training—to include higher-education institutions—that not so long ago was known simply as "diversity training." It has been called other things over the years, some even suitable for printing in this book. The earlier version of what we now know as DEI was designed to fit the law of the land (Civil Rights Act of 1964, Title VII, etc.), and compliance was the order of the day. But that train went off the tracks years ago, and we were left with a fountain-gushing divisiveness across our great land.

DEI evolved into one of the worst purveyors of reverse discrimination ever conceived in America. And that's what we're going to talk about in this chapter: what DEI has done to contribute heavily to rampant divisiveness in this country and the factors that led to its present death throes, killed by executive orders and court decisions. However, some companies have already jettisoned their DEI offices and officers, presumably out of fear of costly lawsuits that would challenge the constitutionality of the programs and their compliance with civil rights laws.

DEI's days of wasting of tens of billions of dollars that have funded this not-so-little cottage industry for years are numbered. The gravy train included healthy salaries to tens of thousands of diversity, equity, and inclusion executives, directors, managers, and rank-and-file employees who are now finding themselves unemployed or in the situation of many workers having to hit the bricks looking for other, more stable jobs. Early birds who saw the handwriting on the wall are now joined by battalions of their compadres as DEI programs continue to be phased out. Finding other employment will not be difficult for the best and brightest who have proven their value to the institution.

We finished our 2023 book *The Adversity of Diversity,* literally, only two weeks after the Supreme Court's affirmative action ruling was announced. The trickle-down effect as it relates to DEI had already started. On July 13, as reported by the *Wall Street Journal*, Republican attorney generals from thirteen states sent a letter to *Fortune* 100 companies (e.g., Coca-Cola, Microsoft, and Johnson & Johnson) warning them against using race-based preferences in hiring, promotions, and contracting. "We urge you to immediately cease any unlawful race-based quotas or preferences your company has adopted for its employment and contracting practices," the letter reportedly said. "If you choose not to do so, know that you will be held accountable."[2]

Although the Supreme Court ruling applied only to the educational component of affirmative action, it was clear to many observers like us that it could eventually be used as precedent for striking down preferential policies in other arenas with legal actions filed to contest the constitutionality or legality (i.e., per the Civil Rights Act of 1964) of workplace affirmative action, which remained in place until Trump placed the kibosh on it.

One of the Cadillacs of DEI-type programs has been the Division of Diversity and Community Engagement (DCE) at the University of Texas in Austin. The publicly funded school reportedly has spent more than $13 million per year floating its DEI program, with almost all of that—$12.2 million—covering the salaries for 171 jobs, according to documents acquired by the *Epoch Times*. Another $1.4 million in pay was spread among fourteen associate deans who comprised what has been known as the Coalition of Diversity, Equity, and Inclusion officers. All this for what has been described as "a contentious sociopolitical movement that has taken hold in America's institutions."[3] Texas taxpayers' money goes beyond the university setting as well. UT Austin's diversity division also funds salaries at what is called the UT Elementary School, which serves pre-K through fifth-grade students as an open-enrollment school.[4]

The University of Texas at Austin had company when it comes to schools forking over big bucks for their DEI-related programs. During the 2021-2022 school year, The Ohio State University paid out $13.4 million for its 132 DEI administrators. At the University of Florida, the figure was believed to be a little over $5 million, which represented just a small piece of the $34 million the entire Florida system reportedly paid out for DEI, although those days might be over. In April 2023, Florida Governor Ron DeSantis, who by then had announced his 2024 run for the presidency, signed legislation defunding DEI in state-run institutions.[5] Texas Governor Greg Abbott soon thereafter signed similar legislation for the state of Texas's higher education programs.

RESISTANCE TO THE 2023 SUPREME COURT RULING

Sherry Sylvester, Distinguished Senior Fellow at the Texas Public Policy Foundation, recognizes the beginning salvos of a war. She has written about the efforts to "defy the law." Valerie Sansone, an assistant professor of higher education at the University of Texas at San Antonio, revealed the secret plan: "Conversations of how to push back are being conducted in hushed tones—not in whispers, but not entirely out in the open either. . . . We're not necessarily using our state university emails to communicate about this. You've got to be a little smarter than that."[6] Sylvester pointed out that, "Sansone and her DEI colleagues in 'the resistance' are fighting the basic premise of all civil rights legislation and the equal protection clause of the Fourteenth Amendment to the Constitution—that there should be no differential treatment in America on the basis of race."

Cracks in the walls of the DEI industry have been popping up in greater frequency over the last few years. You might say the DEI rubber band that has been stretched to its limit in recent years to accommodate Marxist-influenced spin-offs such as BLM, wokeness, CRT, affirmative action, and other openly anti-white organizations and movements, is starting to snap back. We've watched and put up with this stuff long enough, even though there still are millions of misguided people left in this country willing to bend and maybe break laws to support this racially divisive abomination (sounds like "Obama nation," right?).

DEI training breeds racism, pure and simple. Its workers and advocates know that, and they don't care that the rest of us know that. They believe they are in total control of this stuff, and that there is nothing the rest of us can do about it. Well, not so fast. Diversity training not only creates negative consequences, but it also creates discomfort for all who must sit through it. DEI further hardens racial attitudes toward it, feeds into the growth of white grievance as a factor in the rise of the alternative right, bolsters rather than lessens the victimization/white privilege narrative, and exposes differences between people (identity politics) versus promoting a healthy, common identity.

Once that rubber band snaps back and whips a few progressives in the face, they will know it is time for their DEI programs (or whatever they will eventually be called) to focus on true, color-blind diversity and inclusion; in other words, the nondiscrimination the law requires. Let's get back to basics.

They will have to abandon their role in the "antiracist" narrative that until now has blamed, accused, chastised, disparaged, threatened, and even physically harmed Whites for every negative thing imaginable. The most prominent wave of kneejerk reverse discrimination came in the wake of the death of George Floyd, which we covered in Chapter 4.

Some of these anti-white shenanigans are so blatantly prejudicial and unprofessional that when you hear about them, you might assume they are fabrications of one of those phony websites that create and publish outrageously false news story as a form of satirical humor. No one is laughing now. Just like the news story that came out in late June 2023 about a former Penn State University English professor suing the school for reverse discrimination, claiming that the school had forced him to instruct students that the English language embodied White supremacy. Almost unbelievable, but true. Zack DePiero, who, fed up with this extreme anti-White freak show, finally walked away from teaching English at Penn State Abington. In his lawsuit, he alleged that his direct supervisor, Liliana Nayden, had supported the belief that "White supremacy exists in the language itself, and, therefore, that the English language itself is 'racist.'"[7]

Furthermore, as presented in DePiero's lawsuit, the school pushed him and other Penn State faculty members to attend and take part in antiracist workshops and training, including one that was titled "White Teachers Are the Problem." There were other similarly absurd charges made in DePiero's lawsuit, all of which combined—and if true—paint Penn State as an institution that is off its rocker. "DePiero told Fox News Digital that he felt the university's approach to diversity and inclusion produced a "cultlike environment where you had this Original Sin.... In this case, I'm white. I need to repent for that sin."[8]

Here's what some numbers are telling us about what's really going on present-day with DEI training programs. According to Washington, DC-based HR Dive, which, as stated in its LinkedIn profile, "provides in-depth journalism and insight into the most impactful news and trends shaping workforce management,"[9] cited a November 2022 survey conducted by ResumeBuilder.com and Pollfish. The survey found that 52 percent of hiring managers employed by a company with a DEI program reported that their company practiced reverse discrimination. This wasn't just any run-of-the-mill survey knocked out with a few dozen phone calls in a single afternoon.

"Of the 1,000 hiring managers surveyed, 873 work for companies with a DEI initiative," HR Dive reported. "Nearly half say they've been told to prioritize diversity over qualifications (although slightly more than half say they weren't told this). About one in six say they've been told to deprioritize white men when evaluating job candidates. A quarter (25 percent) strongly believe, and 28 percent somewhat believe, they could lose their job if they don't hire enough diverse candidates. More than 600 of the managers surveyed identify as White, according to the survey data."[10]

Hiring employees to fulfill the mission of improving diversity numbers doesn't address one problem DEI managers and specialists are facing—job security. In the early weeks and months following the death of George Floyd, business leaders were bullied by the likes of BLM into ramping up their DEI programs and diversity hiring at breakneck speed, although what any of that had to do with bringing Floyd back to life or making up in any way for the isolated act of a white Minneapolis cop's poor, fatal decision is anyone's guess. No matter, five years after Floyd's death touched off a nationwide glut of rash, frantic C-level moves that were more about social appeasement than common sense and bottom-line responsibility, DEI programs are on thin ice. Diversity hiring has slowed in recent years, and minority hires (just like many of their White fellow employees) are losing their jobs as large corporations on down to smaller businesses make layoffs. Why should DEI program managers, officers, and their own rank and file be exempt from mass layoffs? Welcome to the real world, folks. You wanted equality (or what you call "equity") and now you get it going out just as you got it while getting in or going up.

REVs. JESSE JACKSON AND AL SHARPTON KEEP A CLOSE WATCH

No discussion of Black activists'-driven shakedowns would be complete without an honorable mention for Revs. Jesse Jackson and Al Sharpton on the subject of applying persuasive pressure to White-led corporations, organizations, sports entities, etc.—especially when high-profile racial issues are involved. It's not like BLM has a patent or monopoly on this stuff. If some sort of concession (such as business owners getting with the program and hiring and promoting more Blacks whenever a black man in the act of being arrested dies at the hands [or under the knee] of a white cop) isn't coming, then perhaps a persuasive comment about boycotts or other stringent measures might do the trick. That is, assuming the right kind of person is doing the asking.

Jackson and Sharpton both are seasoned veterans of how this works, occasionally turning up like bad pennies when there is a high-profile, racially connected event or incident begging their intercession and "mediation" skills. When duty calls, with any luck, there is a healthy honorarium, contribution, or perhaps even a "tithe" or "offering" awaiting the inevitable "sales pitch" accompanied by woke's version of passing the plate. Terms (not ours) such as "race baiter"[11] and "shakedown"[12] have been used to describe Jackson's and Sharpton's respective *modi operandi*.

There's a story here. Jeanne Hedgepeth, at the time a Chicago-area high school teacher, in 2021 posted a social media comment in which she called Jackson and Sharpton "race baiters" while also criticizing the rioting that ensued after George Floyd's death, describing the violence as a "civil war." Elsewhere in her post, she also had the audacity to compare the progressives' use of the term "white privilege" to everyone else's use of the N-word. And for that, Hedgepeth was fired from her job, after which she filed a federal lawsuit against officials and board members affiliated with the school district in which she had taught.[13] It would seem freedom of speech—even freedom of *reasonable* speech, in Hedgepeth's case—has no place in parts of Chicago, which just happens to be one of Barack Obama's former hometowns. Does that surprise you?

Both NASCAR and the National Football League, vanguard organizations of the sports world, can vouch for the Jackson/Sharpton factor. According to Kenneth R. Timmerman, author of *Shakedown: Exposing the Real Jesse Jackson*, it was Peter Flaherty, president of the conservative National Legal and Policy Center (based in Washington, DC), who in the early 2000s first brought to light that Jackson had allegedly pressured NASCAR his concern about the lack of success of its black drivers on the stock-car circuit. Nervous about a possible Jackson-inspired boycott, NASCAR reportedly ponied up $250,000 in sponsorship fees for Jackson's groups to get the good reverend to walk away.[14]

Some twenty years later, Sharpton got his turn to play sports-league overlord when the NFL got hit with a lawsuit from former Miami Dolphins coach Brian Flores. A black coach, Flores alleged there is an underlying culture of racism within the league that blocks black coaches from getting head-coaching jobs. In response, the NFL began studying alternatives to its long-standing Rooney Rule, which requires teams to interview at least one minority applicant whenever looking to fill a head-coaching vacancy. Sharpton was one of several civil rights leaders who met with NFL Commissioner Roger Goodell to discuss more effective options to the Rooney Rule, with Sharpton suggesting racial quotas with deadlines, saying the league "must have firm targets and timetables." This coming from a "civil rights leader" who has "incited antisemitic riots and pushed fake hate crimes before they became a popular hoax topic," according to a report in the *Washington Examiner*.[15]

You get the picture. Such has been the state of racial equality in America. It has not been in good hands.

Meanwhile, back in workplaces across America, some see these "sweeping layoffs" of DEI staffers and diversity hires made to improve the numbers as a phenomenon whereby companies are reneging on promises made in the chaotic aftermath of the Floyd killing, and there is a Republican backlash involved as well. That's what reliably liberal mouthpiece news.bloomberglaw.com has been reporting: Workplace diversity and inclusion efforts adopted in the wake of George Floyd's death and ensuing protests are fading as "sweeping layoffs blunt companies' bold commitments to boost underrepresented groups in their C-suites and ranks," reporter Khorri Atkinson wrote in a March 2023 piece under the headline "Corporate Diversity Pledges Fizzle Amid Layoffs, GOP Backlash." He added, "More than 300 DEI professionals departed companies in the last six months including Amazon.com Inc., Twitter Inc., and Nike Inc.," according to a February 2023 report done by Revelio Labs, a workforce analytics firm. "These diminishing roles have left observers questioning whether the sense of urgency to create workforce diversity that corporate leaders made almost three years ago was genuine or simply a reactionary business decision to mitigate reputational risk."[16]

It was in all probability more of the latter.

Corporate leaders—no question—proverbially knocked over office furniture while jumping through hoops to make a good showing during the ruckus that followed Floyd's death. In the court of public opinion, they had no choice at the time. But now that these same corporate leaders are faced, as usual, with pinched dollars in a tightened economy amid the realization that their DEI programs really are fostering a growth of reverse discrimination alongside a decline in available capital, it was time to cut bait. This sort of thing happens across all industries in the corporate world—it's called "rightsizing," and across the board it can be detrimental to everyone's job security. Get used to it, even though you don't have to like it.

Think about it: Why should DEI staffers—or Blacks and other workers from underrepresented groups in general—be exempt from downsizings/layoffs when market conditions or other factors are forcing the hands of company leaders to let workers go? As is often expressed at such unfortunate times in coarser language that most Americans can understand, "stuff" happens. Job (in)security-related anxiety weighs heavily on the minds of workers across the board, regardless of race, creed, faith, gender, etc. It's a fact of life, and blaming and bullying businesses into enacting reverse discrimination policies isn't going to change that.

NO ONE IS IMMUNE

Here's one truth about the DEI industry, which is vulnerable to the same sort of vagaries, ups, and downs that all other industries face from time to time during the constant ebb and flow of commerce—no one is immune. Sometimes you win and get a boost; sometimes you lose and pink slips go out. DEI got its boost after Floyd's death, and BLM, etc. were suddenly empowered to make big demands helped by the compliant mainstream media; now that worm has turned, so to speak.

Let's face it: DEI, at least how it is perceived by its many detractors, has been a front for the woke industry. George Floyd died in the presence and hands of police and then, suddenly, corporations had to make it a top priority to beef up their DEI programs (Note: DEI job listings grew by more than 123 percent in 2020 in the immediate aftermath of the Floyd-related political and racial unrest[17]) and hiring more underrepresented workers. What's the connection there? What does Floyd's death—or his life, for that matter— have to do with workplace staffing dynamics?

Again, those companies and corporations cutting their DEI programs were doing so because they knew those programs and training were useless. All they really accomplished was to keep conflict going because that's exactly what their job was, even though, of course, you would never see that written in a mission statement or annual report. If heterosexuals and homosexuals, and Whites and Blacks and Hispanics, got along, there would be no need for a diversity officer. That's because all they know how to bring to the table is conflict that accused Whites of being White supremacists, or heterosexuals of being homophobes, just by their very existence. If you were born White in this woke world, you were born a racist; no ifs, ands, or buts. What an insane world!

The DEI juggernaut is fraying around the edges; that's even before we got into the increased threat of lawsuits against workplace-diversity manipulations. Contributing to DEI's demise are the cracks we are now seeing with BLM. Its Marxist roots are being revealed more and more, bit by bit, and its questionable accounting practices and spending (tens of millions of dollars reportedly unaccounted for) are apparently putting it on the fast track toward bankruptcy, as covered earlier in this book.[18] Why does the financial health and bold presence of BLM even get mentioned here in the same breath as DEI? It is because BLM is, in a sense, an outside agency that has acted as the enforcement arm of DEI, giving business leaders pause and perhaps a proverbial kick from behind whenever they might have thought that a watered-down diversity program would suffice for their corporations, companies, and organizations. And if BLM has been an enforcer keeping business leaders accountable and in check, much of the mainstream media has been the public-relations agency that kept liberal entities in the headlines, providing a positive spin on such entities as DEI, as needed.

The Court's decision to eliminate the educational component of affirmative action, while not then directly affecting workplace DEI/affirmative action programs and practices, encouraged legal challenges. Morrison Foerster Law Firm wrote in a March 2023 advisory it sent out to its clients, three months ahead of the Court's announcement of its 6-3 decision. "Depending on the Court's reasoning," the firm's advisory continued, "the importance of diversity as a compelling interest more broadly could be impacted and might indirectly undercut some of the rationales used to support DEI initiatives and affirmative action measures in the workplace. As a result, employers should understand the differences between permissible and potentially unlawful DEI and affirmative action programs."[19] Okay, that last part was true, but it did not insulate business leaders from the court of public opinion, which can be swayed by intense public pressures. That, of course, included major squeezes put on business leaders by threats (e.g., threats of boycotts, or worse) from race-based or other minority activist groups such as LGBTQ+ demanding favoritism with their hiring, promotion, retail-oriented, etc. decisions when they hit the streets demanding it, such as what transpired post-Floyd.

WHY DO DIVERSITY PROGRAMS FAIL?

Theories abound as to why diversity programs—such as DEI or as it was referred to until recent years as simply Diversity and Inclusion (DI)—have stumbled or just outright failed. A 2021 *Forbes EQ* commentary highlighted four reasons for DEI's relative failure:

> 1. No long-range plan ("ineffective alignment of the long-term D&I program goals with the organizational strategic plan creates gaps in program delivery and affects sustainability"); 2. Lack of commitment to the program ("If the program is not enforced and modeled by leadership, employees will lack the motivation to buy-in."); 3. Poor instructional delivery model (leaving "the employees lacking in understanding the significance of the new information presented to them."); and 4. Lack of representation ("Everyone must have a seat at the table.").[20]

Of course, we presume that the author of that piece would agree that Whites, Jews, and other non-minority groups have places reserved for them at that table. Also, we are certain that DEI advocates, to be just and fair, would insist that any incendiary race-targeted terms such as "White privilege" and "White supremacy" should be scrubbed from any language used in DI/DEI training and seminars. (Note the sarcasm.)

Until George Floyd's death sent corporate executives, business owners, DEI managers, etc. into knee-jerk, scurrying-around mode attempting to appease the likes of BLM with bolstered DEI efforts, diversity training had for years been focused on compliance to avoid lawsuits. That's what it was all about—do just enough to stay out of court and avoid humongous settlements. That brings us back to what we mentioned earlier: diversity training aimed to curtail bias in the workplace; hiring tests and performance review ratings aimed at mitigating signs of bias in recruiting and job promotions; and grievance processes to give employees an open door to challenge managers on diversity issues: "Those tools are designed to preempt lawsuits by policing managers' thoughts and actions," Frank Dobbin and Alexandra Kalev wrote in their comprehensive study on diversity training that was published in a 2016 edition of *Harvard Business Review*. "Yet laboratory studies show that this kind of force-feeding can activate bias rather than stamp it out. As social scientists have found, people often rebel against rules to assert their autonomy. Try to coerce me to do X, Y, or Z, and I'll do the opposite just to prove that I'm my own person."[21]

After explaining in detail why typical mandatory diversity programs often offer poor returns, Dobbin and Kalev examined a number of alternative approaches to diversity that more effective programs were utilizing—a common element to their success being a more positive framework. "The most effective programs spark engagement, increase contact among different groups, or draw on people's strong desire to look good to others," they commented while zeroing in on several types of programs that seem to work well, such as those that emphasize voluntary training, self-managed teams, cross training (exposing managers to a variety of groups of people instead of favoring one or another), college recruitment targeting women, college recruiting targeting minorities (focusing on historically Black schools), mentoring, and diversity task forces (promoting social accountability and encouraging members to bring solutions back to their respective departments).[22]

The kind of diversity training that Dobbin and Kalev describe—placing positivity over finger pointing—does exist in some workplaces and other organizations that endorse teamwork and managers and employees working toward a common goal, while striving for solutions instead of blame. One company that has steered itself away from being dependent on a formal in-house DEI program is FrankCrum, a professional employer organization (PEO) company that has been around more than forty years. It provides businesses with such services as payroll and human resources (HR) administration, employee benefits/retirement, workers' comp and safety, and HR risk mitigation and employment practices liability insurance (EPLI). I (Carol) spoke with FrankCrum's vice president of human resources, David Peasall, in 2021 about his company's DEI awareness and management:

> I've listened to several DEI trainings . . . It seems the action message was that I need to survey my own employees to find out and document who has what sexual identities and preferences, understand everyone's race and ethnicity, and then make changes. It was very difficult to understand next steps. I'm asking myself, "I'm to ask employees what, exactly? And why would they tell me?" There are laws and common-sense business practices against making employment decisions based on personal characteristics versus objective good business reasons, and for the past fifty-plus years we've been trained that these topics are none of the employer's business. So, now I'm to make it my business and find out this personal information? And this will increase sales and our company's performance?

Peasall also volunteered how FrankCrum isn't about trying to force healthy work environments; it is more about nurturing them. There is a lesson here that DEI proponents could learn:

> Today we talk about 'safe' environments for employees to be in. I see it safer for them to know they can come to work and not be subjected to divisive and polarizing political and social topics. You can come to work and not worry about whether or not to participate, and your manager's perception of you for not participating, in groups formed to talk about feelings and personal information about social, religious, or political topics. That sounds like a good recipe for making people feel divided from each other and distracted from the job they're paid to perform. If they do want to be involved in these topics, they can go on social media and be part of a group outside of work, meeting with their friends and neighbors. But if we're going to respect each other's opinions here at work, we aren't going to spend time on this. Instead, we'll join together to be focused on the mission of the work and how that purpose unites all of us in a common way.

One thing is clear: What the world needs now is to be prepared to talk about what happens after affirmative action, and how DEI programs in higher education never advanced racial healing or reconciliation. What they have done is support segregation and resegregation because they've endorsed having separate dorms, separate class sections, separate this, separate that. They've been divisive. People in the corporate world need to know that students who were educated under that system of DEI took their values into the corporate world. Consequently, instead of corporations being able to focus on the profits and the mission of the founders and owners, they have had to address historical injustices identified by the diversity regime.

IDENTITY POLITICS HARD AT WORK

The problem with diversity and anti-bias programs have been the one-shoe-fits-all approach that comes with some pretty dangerous baggage. DEI has encouraged individuals to go into companies and organizations that are expected to affirm their group identities with affinity groups that in some cases devolve into grievance sessions that produce unreasonable demands that take CEOs and supervisors from the business of business. This should be expected because DEI and CRT emerged from a Marxist framework geared toward stoking conflict and hostility between oppressors and those deemed members of oppressed groups. Reconciliation and healing can never take place in an environment that divides workers and takes them away mentally and physically from the jobs they were hired to do.

We believe America is headed in the right direction. What we need is an alternative to the kinds of workplace exercises and programs that have pitted women against men and minorities against members of the dominant group. We believe we have a solution to all this that can help heal America, and it's called unity training—not the divisive diversity training we have grown accustomed to encountering. Carol Swain's REAL Unity Training Solutions offers an off-ramp for institutions that want to do the right thing within the legal framework provided by the U.S. Civil Rights Act and the Constitution's equal protection clause. We believe knowledge is power and that everyone should be treated with respect and dignity in the workplace. The days of pitting workers against one another because of politics or immutable characteristics must end once and for all.

CHAPTER 6

REAL Unity Training Solutions: An Antidote to DEI's Divisiveness

> "*Eliminating racial discrimination means eliminating all of it. And the equal protection clause, we have accordingly held, applies 'without regard to any differences of race, of color, or of nationality'—it is 'universal in [its] application.' . . . For '[t]he guarantee of equal protection cannot mean one thing when applied to one individual and something else when applied to a person of another color.' . . If both are not accorded the same protection, then it is not equal.*"[1]
> — **U.S. Supreme Court Chief Justice John Roberts**, Majority Opinion, June 2023, *Students for Fair Admissions v. President and Fellows of Harvard College*

> "*While I am painfully aware of the social and economic ravages which have befallen my race and all who suffer discrimination, I hold out enduring hope that this country will live up to its principles so clearly enunciated in the Declaration of Independence and the Constitution of the United States: that all men are created equal, are equal citizens, and must be treated equally before the law.*"[2]
> — **U.S. Supreme Court Justice Clarence Thomas**, Concurring Opinion, June 2023, *Students for Fair Admissions v. President and Fellows of Harvard College.*

ALTHOUGH BOTH U.S. SUPREME COURT CHIEF JUSTICE JOHN ROBERTS AND JUSTICE CLARENCE THOMAS (above) were addressing the Court's 6-3 verdict to strike down race as a factor to be used in college admissions, their words could just as well have applied to the state of workplace DEI programs and training. That is another place where equal protection has been shelved such that one segment of the population (Blacks, Hispanics, women, and members of the LGBTQ+ population) have received preferential treatment, and another segment (heterosexual white men, Christians, and Asians) have found themselves disparaged and left feeling alienated. That has begun to change because of the executive orders and the dominoes falling from the 2023 Court decision and Trump's January 2025 EOs.

Before we get to the birth of REAL Unity Training Solutions and its vision of diversity without discrimination, let us also go back nearly twenty years to 2004. That's when Barack Obama, then a member of the Illinois State Senate, gave a keynote speech at the Democratic National Convention that stirred the hearts and minds of his fellow Democrats and parts of the rest of the nation. It was a well-written speech and delivered to perfection, a classic; Obama read it aloud well. His speech not only essentially launched his quest to the White House, it also unwittingly (to him, apparently) included a segment that could be interpreted as contrarian to the divisiveness that has been wrought in today's model of diversity training. It is a model in which black and white nations separately exist, the former being the beneficiary of a form of preferential treatment that seemingly violates the U.S. Constitution; the latter has been victimized by reverse discrimination while being disparaged as purveyors of "White privilege" and "White supremacy."

Let us show you what we mean. Here's an outtake from Obama, speaking at the 2004 Democratic National Convention:

E Pluribus Unum. Out of Many, One.

Now even as we speak, there are those who are preparing to divide us, the spin masters, the negative ad peddlers who embrace the politics of anything goes. Well, I say to them tonight, there is not a liberal America and a conservative America—there is the United States of America. There is not a Black America and a White America and Latino America and Asian America—there's the United States of America. . . .

I stand here today, grateful for the diversity of my heritage, aware that my parents' dreams live on in my two precious daughters. I stand here knowing that my story is part of the larger American story, that I owe a debt to all of those who came before me, and that, in no other country on earth is my story even possible.[3]

REAL UNITY TRAINING SOLUTIONS: AN ANTIDOTE TO DEI'S DIVISIVENESS

When he was an llinois state senator Barack Obama spoke words that Americans wanted and needed to hear. The man who mesmerized the world in 2004 certainly would not be at all in favor of how diversity, equity, and inclusion training has evolved in the 2020s. We know what he appeared to be was not actually who he was.

I (Carol) remember the speech vividly. In fact, I wrote an essay for *Ebony* magazine that was published in December 2006. Not only did I say America was ready for a black president, I wrote: "The first successful black candidate will be a person like Barack Obama or Gen. Colin Powell, both of whom embody the American dream."[4]

Obama and I seemingly shared a deep appreciation for *E Pluribus Unum*—it is the foundation for my REAL Unity Training Solutions, LLC, which grew from an idea I birthed during the summer of 2020. Over the past two years, I have been observing American politics and developing what I believe is a better approach to healing group conflicts, especially between Whites and Blacks. So in one sense, Obama (or at least the version of him who spoke so eloquently and inspirationally twenty-one years ago) and I had one thing in common—we did not want to see a separate Black America and White America (which is what DEI had been striving to give us). We preferred one unified nation where diversity can be pursued and celebrated instead of weaponized in pitting one segment of America against the other. Unfortunately, the Obama who assumed the presidency in 2008 bore little resemblance to the man we adored in 2004.

We now know that race-based solutions that discriminate against Whites and Asians had to be tackled and could not continue to exist. The trickle-down effects of the Court's landmark 2023 decision affecting colleges and universities had implications for the workplace. We saw those effects start to occur almost immediately. The uptake is that American institutions and corporations must now rethink how they approach anti-bias training and continuing education for supervisors and their underlings. Civil rights laws and the Equal Protection Clause of the Fourteenth Amendment governs how CEOs, owners, and employees should interact with one another and the populations served if they are to avoid federal lawsuits and bad publicity because of employee ignorance of the law. Otherwise, the workplace will become a tinder keg given that there are laws to be followed and best practices instituted if lawsuits and bad publicity are to be avoided. Unity of mission and purpose are worthy goals for all to pursue.

THE BIRTH OF REAL UNITY TRAINING SOLUTIONS

The spark for REAL Unity Training Solutions—and the seed that would later blossom into *The Adversity for Diversity*—ignited in the fall of 2020, amid a nation reeling from George Floyd's death earlier that year in Minneapolis. I was invited by the Council on National Policy to speak on a panel about race relations, just months after protests and riots had gripped cities nationwide. The event was a private, off-the-record discussion, but a *Washington Post* reporter slipped into the audience and recorded some of our remarks.[5] I had argued that conservatives needed to step into the diversity, equity, and inclusion (DEI) arena—not to mimic the prevailing models, but to challenge them. I saw businesses across America shelling out big money for DEI consultants who, in my view, sowed disruption while offering little real progress on race or gender relations. That moment planted a seed: there had to be a better way.

My motivation deepened as I watched the country wrestle with nightly riots, corporate virtue signaling, and a flood of funds pouring into Black Lives Matter and DEI programs. I felt a heavy burden for our nation. Every headline seemed to scream division—crime spiked, law enforcement was vilified, and companies funneled millions to activists and figures such as Ibram X. Kendi and Robin DiAngelo, seemingly more to appease the mob than to heal anything. I couldn't shake the conviction that racial reconciliation wouldn't come from a conflict-driven, cultural Marxist framework. Then, one restless night, the word "unity" jolted me awake. As a Christian, I felt it in my spirit: unity was the antidote to this growing divisiveness. I raced to my computer and searched for "Unity Training," only to discover that the domain name I wanted was gone. So I decided to name my company "Unity Training Solutions." In October 2020, I registered it as a single-member limited liability corporation. It became a living, breathing organization birthed with a vision to restore workplaces to their core missions and free from the chaos of identity politics and managing grievance related to the historic wrongs that DEI experts constantly harped on.

Unity Training Solution rejected and refused to borrow from the Marxist-based and flawed research methods of DEI programs I saw popping up everywhere. They were claiming falsely to be about unity (more than five hundred trademark applications for "unity"-named ventures were pending when I sought to trademark my company). Checking boxes or guilting employees into compliance can never be part of a unity vision. After discovering the Left's embrace of the "unity" concept, I made a decision to rebrand my organization. It became Carol Swain's REAL Unity Training Solutions. We have evolved a great deal since Fall 2020. We have gone beyond addressing issues of education and now work with nonprofits and government employees. REAL Unity Training Solutions' aim was to arm leaders with practical, principle-driven tools—grounded in my knowledge and experiences after decades as a political science and law professor, and my service on the U.S. Civil Rights Commission. My vision is to see organizations and corporations that have gone astray to refocus on teamsmanship and respect for every individual. The golden rule became my guide: treat others as you'd want to be treated, no scapegoating, no shaming. Organizations veering off course, distracted by social agendas, needed an off-ramp—a way back to their founding purposes, where diversity strengthens rather than divides. That is where my heart lies on the matter. DEI and affirmative action are in their death throes, but companies and organizations need assistance for the foreseeable future as they work their way through change.

EQUIPPING CEOs AND LEADERS

REAL Unity Training Solutions has evolved into an approach that focuses on equipping CEOs and other leaders rather than attempting the impossible task of trying to change the culture of an organization. It is the role of the leader or CEO to set the tone for their organization. We want to help leaders get back to the basics of running an organization without having to deal with the distractions and conflict that the DEI approach dumped into the workplace. DEI inevitably creates unrest and discord when it divides the workplace into warring affinity groups. Our goal is to equip CEOs and owners with information on how they can attain a healthy form of diversity without reaping divisiveness; how they can restore equal opportunity without the false promise of equity's equal outcomes; and how they can accomplish integration without having to address group demands for a form of inclusion that saw affinity groups proliferate. Identity groups often lead to self-segregation, where participants end up griping about their workplaces or learning environments rather than focusing on their purpose for being at the organization.

We at REAL Unity Training respect the autonomy of the individual and believe that talent is distributed across the human spectrum without special regard to race, sex, religion, or sexual orientation. What should matter is the skill, attitudes, and dedication of individuals to the mission and purpose of the organization. Focusing on the mission of the organization is a critically important part of getting back to the basics. The end result is a common-sense approach done within the confines of civil rights laws and constitutional protections.

Along those lines, there is plenty of room for improvement in how training is conducted in America, and, as touched on in chapter 5, there is a variety of great ideas begging to be implemented by fair-minded managers. Even staunchly Left-leaning advocates have come to the realization that bullying Whites and directing phony blame at them—especially white males—are counterproductive tactics that are failing to achieve the kind of diversity, equality, and inclusion that all of us can agree are beneficial to all groups.

Organizations can never bring about reconciliation using a conflict model. With the type of workplace diversity training we have seen in recent years, its proponents cannot point to any successes; at least not authentic ones, just false narratives to support the continuation of conflict-based DEI. Diversity was a more laudable goal when its proponents adhered to the original civil rights goals of nondiscrimination and equal opportunity; that was before identity politics took on its sharp edge. It was not long after the passage of the civil rights action that blatantly reverse discrimination and group entitlement to the extreme reared their heads in far flung organizations.

I (Carol) can attest to the fact that the Civil Rights Movement helped people like me, for whom doors were opened. We were given an opportunity to prove ourselves in an environment where we had an equal opportunity to succeed or fail. That all seems like ancient history now. I believe if we go back to the original intent, the original premise, the original vision of affirmative action as created by President John F. Kennedy and augmented by President Lyndon Johnson in the sixties, we land at the Civil Rights Act of 1964 which prohibited group discrimination and sought to use outreach, nondiscrimination, and advertising to reach underrepresented persons who previously experienced discrimination because of their immutable characteristics. Most Americans were certainly on board with the strides we made toward achieving a color-blind society. We were equal under the law, but individual prejudices and biases continued to exist in the hearts of men and women. That is human nature. We had to learn to get along and respect each other as individuals, not as members of discrete groups.

CUSTOMIZED TRAINING BASED ON NEEDS

REAL Unity offers customized training based on the needs of the organization as defined by its CEO and owner(s), who presumably are in the best position to decide where their company or organization needs to go to achieve their bottom-line goals. Carol Swain's REAL Unity Training Solutions is intended to replace and certainly improve on the one size-fits-all model that most DEI-equipped companies advocate—the one that has morphed into something unrecognizable when placed alongside what the presidential executive orders for affirmative action, the Civil Rights Act of 1964, equal opportunity, and even the U.S. Constitution together laid out as a path to constructive diversity.

Much of the diversity training I am aware of uses a one-size-fits-all model for tackling issues involving groups deemed historically marginalized: women, racial and ethnic minorities, and members of the LGBTQ+ communities. Too many DEI trainers come across as angry individuals who show open hostility toward groups considered privileged. A better approach is one that is customized for the organization; it should begin with the vision of the owner and founder which ties into the company's reason for existence. Workplace assessments are important. That is because, in some cases, there are no problems until the DEI officers or trainers arrive with their push for mandatory indoctrination. In some cases, there might not be any DEI-related issues at the company or organization, and if it is not broken, there is nothing to be fixed. Like the old saying goes, "If it ain't broke, don't fix it." (You'll only make things worse.)

It is critical for leaders and supervisors to know the civil rights laws of the land so that workers can be informed and lawsuits avoided. We believe the current approach is a failure and that there is no need or benefit to temporarily take employees off the job, even for less than a day, to be coached by DEI instructors. We have heard of situations where someone internally pushed for a sensitivity or DEI coach to be brought into the organization where employees were forced to attend. What sometimes happens is the workplace is left worse off. Workers who were previously satisfied with their jobs and with their work environment end up leaving. That kind of voluntary attrition does not make your company more genuinely diverse or more successful, assuming you measure success by the bottom line. If your diversity percentages are up, but your bottom line is bottoming out and workforce departures outpace the new hires, you have a problem. In such a divisive environment, Whites might feel like they have been singled out and beaten up; minorities might feel like they've gotten the worst end of a bad deal, and that they should be further along in their careers than they are. DEI is a lose-lose proposition.

Even if you really stretch things and cast DEI—at least as it is being practiced in 2025—in a positive light, assessing and attempting to discuss its value nonetheless stymies business leaders and human resource executives and managers across the board. Even rank-and-file employees see a fuzzy picture regardless of their viewpoint. For instance, the *Wall Street Journal* in a July 2023 piece mentions Clayton Homes, a Tennessee-based builder of mobile and modular homes that employs about 26,000 workers. About half of those employees claim the company's diversity measures don't, well, measure up; the other half say those diversity protocols go too far, implying those measures are unfair to them.

"There are people who say, 'I really wish we were more diverse,' and I've also seen people say, 'Stop being so woke,' " says Sarah Sharp, a human resources vice president at Clayton. She also pointed out how she is attempting to enhance objectivity when it comes to hiring, her aim being to attract and promote more underrepresented people while at the same time expressing these initiatives in a manner of language that shows overall fairness.[6]

Also cited by the *Wall Street Journal* is a growing trend in which white men say they are taking it on the chin in the workplace, no thanks to diversity programs and measures. "Jonathan McBride, a global managing partner who leads the DEI practice for recruiting firm Heidrick & Struggles, says the companies he works with worry about alienating some workers and say feelings of belonging are dropping among white men, as shown in internal surveys," *WSJ* reporters Te-Ping Chen and Ray A. Smith wrote. Likewise, research conducted by a unit of executive search firm Spencer Stuart found that more than half of white men surveyed reported not being valued at work or were "not given full credit for their contributions."[7]

In the wake of the Supreme Court's June 2023 decision to remove race as a factor in college admissions, workplaces were placed on notice—the handwriting was on the wall. Companies must now work more diligently in preparing their employees by informing them about civil rights laws. Knowledge is not only power, but can also be a source of unity, bringing people together.

A core value of unity training is treating other people with respect regardless of which group they belong to. Like we stated earlier, though, it also means that you are not celebrating one group of people's special day at the exclusion of other groups' special days. Other than major holidays, it is probably best to celebrate no one group's special day and to end the preachy nonstop emails that come from DEI's influence on human resources offices. Unity training is about making sure the workplace is a place where, when you are on the clock, you are focused on the mission of the organization, not on catering to or pandering to the social or cultural distinctions of a particular group. Along with that, diversity training and management should not be part of some sort of social engineering platform. It should be a place where people come to do a job and work as a team around the goals of the organization. That is not difficult to grasp.

A HISTORY LESSON IS IN ORDER

It bears repeating that people need to know the history of our nation and our civil rights laws against discrimination. Workers should be educated about the laws of the land that affect how they should interact with one another; that goes beyond just lawsuit avoidance. There is nothing wrong with that kind of training, except we don't see much of that. In fact, that is what *honest* unity training should do—educate leaders and managers about the laws of the land and the history of civil rights; then make it clear to them that civil rights protect everyone, including men and Whites. Beyond the basics, we then need to be reminded of the wisdom of leaders such as Stephen Covey, who authored the classic book *The Seven Habits of Highly Effective People*[8] and the impressive work of Patrick Lencioni, author of T*he Five Dysfunctions of a Team*.[9] At the end of the day, leaders and CEOs need guidance and a work environment that, to the extent possible, avoids direct engagement in the shifting politics of the day.

The reverse discrimination promoted by race-based diversity training and affirmative action stigmatizes the accomplishments of racial and ethnic minorities who are high achieving. Everyone's hard work and earned accomplishments can be discounted as a by-product of race-based policies. Once again, to reinforce where we are coming from, we believe companies would have a better work environment if more people knew and practiced the Golden Rule. If it is wrong to discriminate against Blacks and Hispanics, it is also wrong to discriminate against Whites. If bullying and shaming is harmful to black and brown children, it is also harmful to white children.

I consider myself an astute observer of the passing parade. I seek to apply common sense to the world around me, and I sometimes see trends before others do. With race-based affirmative action, I saw the problems years ago when I authored my book *The New White Nationalism in America: Its Challenge to Integration*.[10] Back in 2002, I saw how identity politics and multiculturalism were dividing Americans in undesirable ways. The result was a rising White consciousness and identification as a discriminated-against group. Our society has moved in a direction where unity is more difficult because fewer people know the Constitution or the lofty vision cast by the Declaration of Independence—even fewer know the Judeo-Christian values that undergirded our nation. What I recognized then—and even more so today—is the dangerous collision course we are on when it comes to race relations and the tribalism of multiculturalism. Our current approach has created a devil's brew for racial conflict and hatred.

Although the days of diversity training that play on identity politics, reverse discrimination, and bashing and disenfranchising white people have been ordered dead via executive orders, change will not happen overnight. That is because many people remain unaware of the dynamic changes that have transpired in America since January 2025 that have thrown everything into flux. We must now focus on what will work in place of racially discriminatory DEI approaches that companies can use to create mobility for talented individuals willing to work hard, grasp, and run with the opportunities that come their way. If CEOs and owners concentrate on the needs of the organization and the skills necessary to perform the task at hand, a nondiscriminatory approach to recruiting and retaining talented individuals will sweep in a lot of people, and some of them will be underrepresented minorities who can work as part of a team.

Treating everyone fairly as an image bearer of God should help bring about the kind of camaraderie that will make for stronger teams composed of individuals with similar talents who genuinely respect each other. Promoting on the basis of merit is what many people want. This is a sure way to get rid of some of that resentment that poor or working-class Whites now hold. The end result is that nondiscrimination and equal opportunity in a mission-focused organization have the potential to return us to the original vision of the civil rights activists. They are the ones who asked for nondiscrimination and *not* for the special privileges that members of protected groups have received that helped create a lot of resentment. Unfortunately, a lot of what progressives have been doing in recent decades have reversed the gains that people—namely minorities to include Blacks—had already made.

It is important to remember that the tenets and original intent of affirmative action and what we now know as DEI are very closely related, in a sense synonymous with one another. It's important to embrace this when examining the overarching influence and outcomes yet to be that will follow the Supreme Court's decision to significantly diminish the use of racial preferences in American universities. A similar fate awaits those who persist in using racial preferences in workplace hiring and promotions, with or without a Supreme Court ruling of its own (yet). In their book, *Mismatch*,[11] Richard Sander and Stuart Taylor Jr. say that such preferences hinder underrepresented minorities far more than they help them. In an online summary of their book, which we first mentioned in chapter 2, the authors go on to explain how "dramatic new data and numerous interviews with affected former students and university officials of color . . . show how racial preferences often put students in competition with far better prepared classmates, dooming many to fall so far behind that they can never catch up. . . . Even though black applicants are more likely to enter college than whites with similar backgrounds, they are far less likely to finish; why there are so few black and Hispanic professionals with science and engineering degrees and doctorates; why black law graduates fail bar exams at four times the rate of Whites; and why universities accept relatively affluent minorities over working class and poor people of all races."[12]

What this tells me, and what I have seen with my own eyes in many college classrooms as student and, later, professor, is that because of affirmative action, many students from underrepresented groups get recruited into Ivy League or other academically elite schools and end up unable to succeed. What I believe ensues is anger and often an embrace of Marxist theories of oppression. This results in protest and activism rather than study and high achievement in some cases. In hindsight, many of the students who graduate at the bottom of their class at an elite institution would have been better off starting out at a state institution where the admissions and academic standards might better match their profile.

GOAL SHOULD BE RACE-NEUTRAL RECRUITMENT

No doubt there have been many minorities over the years who have been destined for success, only to end up recruited into situations that put them in over their heads from their start, and from that it is difficult to recover. With race-neutral recruitment, support from professors and grad students, remedial help where needed (math for me when I was in school), and just understanding the circumstances that people come from, schools and students can succeed and advance. They can get good jobs for which they will be properly suited without the crutch of a system that focused on group membership and less so on individual accomplishments. People will thrive when they are in the right environment. Unfortunately, affirmative action programs placed a stigma on every racial and ethnic minority, so much so that we experienced a Biden administration where high-profile leaders touted their group identities rather than their qualifications for the job. Whether they knew it or not, their presence in a position attained through identity group politics hurt every qualified member of their group, individuals who worked their butts off to attain their positions. The only important factor should be one's qualifications for a position and how well they perform. Membership in a historically disadvantaged group should be irrelevant in most situations. It should neither advantage or disadvantage anyone.

Targeting any special group or labeling them as evil or deficient because they are male, or because they are white or Asian, should not be the goal of an effective training program. Civil rights laws protect individuals. We should be searching for diamonds in the rough and talented people who want to work hard at bettering themselves while taking advantage of opportunities offered on a nonracial or nongender basis. A successful training program zeroes in on the mission as originally expressed—and presumably still applicable present-day for leaders of the organization. In its optimal application, it should bring together employees around a mission without singling out or denigrating any group. Fear should not prevent leaders from standing strong and doing the right thing rather than the trendy thing for their organization. WorldBlu, founded by Traci Fenton, is a prime example of a leadership organization that helps business owners and CEOs move beyond fear toward freedom to innovate and build a healthy organizational democracy within the workplace that advances the mission of the institution.[13]

REAL Unity Training Solutions believes that the secret to building strong teams is respecting and harnessing individual talent. Our goal is to help leaders of corporations, businesses, nonprofits, religious institutions, and other organizations achieve their goals by providing viable alternatives to the divisive and counterproductive critical race and gender theories that have divided Americans and disrupted institutions. We respect everyone's civil rights and equality under the law. We encourage Americans to rediscover and re-embrace our national motto: *E Pluribus Unum* (out of many, one). We also encourage other companies with a similar vision to compete in this space because knowledge is power, and the system is so broken that no single company could meet the needs of all. We encourage leaders and CEOs to have the courage and freedom to explore new and better ways of helping their organization become the best they can be while harnessing and developing the human capital entrusted to them as leaders who lead by example and not by fear and intimidation.

Following are Real Unity Training Solutions' twelve core values, in no particular order:

Core Values and Principles
- We want institutions to succeed.
- We believe unity is positive and productive.
- We believe the citizens of our nation share more similarities than differences.
- We respect the differences of others.
- We care about justice and fairness.
- We believe that customer service should be a top priority.
- We believe in traditional "success principles" of hard work, integrity, and accountability.
- We have no hidden agendas.
- We are truthful with our clients and our team.
- We believe in transparency and honest dialogue.
- We are financially responsible.
- We accept personal responsibility for our results.[*]

Unity training involves common sense, understanding the Constitution and the law; respecting and being tactful with one another; working as teams and celebrating the victories, big and small; encouraging one another; and being an active listener and observer, all at the same time all the time. There are numerous challenges and obstacles lurking to prevent you from being able to pull this off—to achieve constructive diversity training without offending anyone. One of the elephants in the room is the rampant divisiveness in our nation, spilling over into the workplace, where there is evidence of "wokeness" around almost every corner. When we interviewed Mike Hardwick, the founder, president, and CEO of Tennessee-based Churchill Mortgage, which

---

[*] This information and more about REAL Unity Training Solutions is also available at our website, www.unitytrainingsolutions.com.

employs eleven hundred workers servicing forty-six states, he brought up the issue of divisiveness. Mike described it in terms that sound an awful lot like a description of wokeness:

"Our [surrounding] culture these days is radically different than it's been for most of my business career," Hardwick said. "There is so much divisiveness in our society today. That's a sad reality. You find yourself checking a lot of your thoughts because you have to be more cautious in how you express yourself. And that's not all bad. Because it goes back to this—when we express our thoughts, shouldn't we do so with respect to everybody? Different opinions, feelings and thoughts are okay, but can't we do that respectfully?

"When people respect each other, they can communicate better with each other, find areas of agreement. There's more peace and harmony through that effort than the railing, hollering, marching, raising banners, cussing that a lot of people tend to do. I don't know that anger has ever produced a lot of good. Respect, patience, seeking to understand others, I have found, works better more often than not."[14]

Let me close by repeating something I said in an October 28, 2022, article that appeared in *The Federalist*. Suitable for this book, the title of that article was "A Plan to Make 'Diversity, Equity, and Inclusion' Die." Exactly.

> I have always believed in America. I'm a product of the American dream. I have had faith in the Constitution, and the Bill of Rights, because that distinguished us from other nations. So there's a part of me that's very troubled at where our nation is at this point in time, but I try to stay optimistic because I believe that whatever we may think separates us, we are Americans at the core and . . . what unites us is far greater than what divides us.[15]

We can have a healthy nation and workplace.

EPILOGUE

The Shifting Sands of DEI and Affirmative Action Since July 2023

WHEN *THE ADVERSITY OF DIVERSITY* WAS FIRST CONCEIVED (in 2023), the landscape of Diversity, Equity, and Inclusion (DEI) and affirmative action stood at a crossroads. The U.S. Supreme Court's landmark decision in *Students for Fair Admissions, Inc. v. President and Fellows of Harvard College*, announced June 29, 2023, struck down race-conscious college admissions, effectively dismantling decades of affirmative action precedent in higher education. This ruling was a seismic shift, one that eventually rippled far beyond university campuses and into corporate boardrooms, government agencies, and public discourse. Nearly two years later, the terrain has shifted dramatically since the Trump EOs. It's a story that continues to unfold with profound implications.

The Supreme Court's decision was a catalyst, emboldening and encouraging conservative activists and lawmakers to target DEI initiatives across multiple sectors. By mid-2023, the ruling had already sparked a wave of legal challenges and corporate reassessments. Companies such as Netflix, Disney, and Warner Bros., which had heavily invested in DEI following the 2020 George Floyd protests, began quietly scaling back. Chief diversity officer roles, which surged by 168.9 percent between 2019 and 2022 according to LinkedIn data, saw a sharp decline in demand.[1] Headhunters reported the lowest interest in these positions in three decades, signaling a retreat from what critics—like Elon Musk, who called DEI "just another word for racism"—had long decried as discriminatory overreach.[2] By early 2025, major corporations such as McDonald's, Ford, and Meta had publicly announced the dissolution of specific DEI programs, citing the 2023 ruling as a legal inflection point.[3]

85

These corporate rollbacks coincided with a broader political assault on DEI, culminating in decisive action under the Trump administration following his January 20, 2025, inauguration. On his first day, President Trump signed an executive order titled "Ending Radical and Wasteful Government DEI Programs and Preferencing," revoking Biden-era mandates such as Executive Order 13985, which had embedded DEI across federal agencies since 2021.[4] The order also axed Lyndon Johnson's 1965 affirmative action mandate (Executive Order 11246), effectively dismantling the Office of Federal Contract Compliance Programs.[5] Federal DEI staff were placed on paid leave, with plans for eventual layoffs, and agencies were directed to purge "equity action plans" and "environmental justice" initiatives. Trump's Department of Government Efficiency (DOGE), led by Elon Musk, took aim at what it called taxpayer-funded "partisan orthodoxy," fingering DEI as an un-American relic of identity politics.[6]

State-level responses mirrored this federal pivot. By March 2025, at least ten states—Alabama, Florida, and Texas among them—had implemented anti-DEI laws banning state funds for diversity programs in public universities and workplaces. Florida's restrictions, championed by Governor Ron DeSantis, went further, targeting private sector DEI training under the "Stop WOKE" Act framework. Meanwhile, universities like the University of Texas and the University of Florida shuttered diversity offices and student programs, complying with new mandates. Critics of these measures, including DEI consultants like Tina Opie, argued that such moves erased decades of progress in addressing systemic inequities.[7] Yet supporters, like Christopher Rufo of the Manhattan Institute, hailed them as a return to meritocracy, asserting that DEI had always been a guise for reverse discrimination.

Despite this backlash, pockets of resistance persist. Corporations with long-standing DEI commitments—think Deloitte UK—have doubled down, emphasizing inclusion over explicit racial preferences to navigate legal risks.[8] Employee Resource Groups (ERGs) and self-care strategies have gained traction as grassroots alternatives to top-down DEI mandates, particularly in organizations weathering the post-2023 chill. On the legal front, the Equal Employment Opportunity Commission maintains that voluntary DEI efforts remain lawful for private employers, though the specter of future Supreme Court rulings looms large.[9] Justice Neil Gorsuch's 2023 concurrence hinted at extending the Harvard decision to workplaces. The EOs banning DEI in

The Shifting Sands of DEI and Affirmative Action Since July 2023

federally supported programs and Trump's EO ending affirmative action totally redefines the landscape for civil rights protections.

Looking ahead, the trajectory of DEI and affirmative action suggests a contentious future. By 2026, we might see the Supreme Court revisit workplace DEI under cases already percolating through lower courts. These include challenges to corporate hiring quotas or race-based training programs that linger. Legal scholars predict that the Court's conservative majority, fortified by its 2023 precedent, could rule that any race-conscious policy—public or private—violates equal protection principles or Title VII, effectively outlawing DEI as we know it.[10] Organizations persisting with these initiatives, particularly in states with aggressive anti-DEI statutes, will likely face a barrage of lawsuits from activist groups like America First Legal, which has pledged to "dismantle the DEI regime" through litigation.

For those defiantly clinging to affirmative action's remnants—universities or employers using proxies like socioeconomic status to preserve racial outcomes—the legal risks are even ominous. Anticipate a wave of class-action suits alleging reverse discrimination, backed by plaintiffs emboldened by the 2023 ruling and funded by conservative donors. States such as Texas and Florida might pioneer civil penalties, fining institutions that skirt bans with creative workarounds. By 2027, DEI could be reduced to a shadow of its former self: a voluntary, race-neutral shell, stripped of enforceable power. *The Adversity of Diversity* foresaw this unraveling—a system buckling under its own contradictions. The question now is not whether DEI and affirmative action will survive, but what will rise from their ashes.

Notes

Preface

1. Carol M. Swain, "Why I'm Celebrating the End of the DEI Era," *Katie Couric Media*, January 27, 2025, https://katiecouric.com/news/opinion/end-of-dei-benefits-carol-swain/
2. Executive Orders, "Ending Radical and Wasteful Government DEI Programs" and "Ending Illegal Discrimination and Restoring Merit-Based Opportunity," President Donald J. Trump, signed January 20-21, 2025.
3. Civil Rights Act of 1964, Pub. L. No. 88-352, 78 Stat. 241; Voting Rights Act of 1965, Pub. L. No. 89-110, 79 Stat. 437; Open Housing Act of 1968, Pub. L. No. 90-284, 82 Stat. 81.
4. Trump executive order, "Ending Illegal Discrimination and Restoring Merit-Based Opportunity," January 2025.
5. Tracy Jan, Jena McGregor, and Meghan Hoyer, "Corporate America's $50 Billion Promise," *Washington Post,* August 21, 2023, https://www.washingtonpost.com/business/interactive/2021/george-floyd-corporate-america-racial-justice/
6. Jeff Green, David Ingold, Raeedah Wahid, Cedric Sam and Daniela Sirtori-Cortina, "Corporate America Promised to Hire a Lot More People of Color. It Actually Did," bloomberg.com, September 26, 2023. https://www.bloomberg.com/graphics/2023-black-lives-matter-equal-opportunity-corporate-diversity/
7. Sundiatu Dixon-Fyle, Kevin Dolan, Dame Vivian Hunt, and Sara Prince, "Diversity Wins: How Inclusion Matters," mckinsey,com, May 19, 2020, https://www.mckinsey.com/featured-insights/diversity-and-inclusion/diversity-wins-how-inclusion-matters.
8. Sara Rumpf-Whitten, "Google, Meta, and Other Tech Giants Slash DEI-Related Jobs, Resource Groups in 2023: Report," foxbusiness.com, December 27, 2023, https://www.foxbusiness.com/technology/google-meta-tech-giants-slash-dei-related-jobs-resource-groups-report.

NOTES

9. Supreme Court ruling on race-based college admissions, 2023, *Students for Fair Admissions, Inc. v. President and Fellows of Harvard College*, 600 U.S. ___ (2023).

10. Jeremiah Green and John Hand, "McKinsey's Diversity Matters/Delivers/Wins Results Revisited," Vol 21, *Econ Journal Watch*, March 2024, pp. 5-34, https://econjwatch.org/articles/mckinsey-s-diversity-matters-delivers-wins-results-revisited.

11. Carol Swain and Mike Towle, *The Adversity of Diversity: How the Supreme Court's Decision to Remove Race from College Admissions Criteria Will Doom Diversity Programs* (Nashville, TN: Be the People Books, 2023).

12. Carol M. Swain, "Lawfare and the Death of Affirmative Action," https://www.foxnews.com/opinion/lawfare-and-the-death-of-dei-and-affirmative-action, February 21, 2025.

13. Lawsuit filed by the National Association of Diversity Officers in Higher Education et al., *National Association of Diversity Officers in Higher Education et al v. Trump et al*, No. 1:2025cv00333 - Document 44 (D. Md. 2025) February 12, 2025.

14. Jean-Baptiste Alphonse Karr, *Les Guêpes*, 1849.

Chapter 1

1. Lyndon B. Johnson, "Commencement Address at Howard University: 'To Fulfill These Rights,'" www.presidency.ucsb.edu, June 4, 1965, https://www.presidency.ucsb.edu/documents/commencement-address-howard-university-fulfill-these-rights

2. U.S. Supreme Court Chief Justice John Roberts, "Majority Opinion: '*Students for Fair Admissions v. President and Fellows of Harvard College*,' " June 29, 2023, https://supreme.justia.com/cases/federal/us/600/20-1199/#tab-opinion-4758916

3. Executive Order 14151: "Ending Radical and Wasteful Government DEI Programs and Preferencing," by President Donald Trump, January 20, 2025; Executive Order 14173: "Ending Illegal Discrimination and Restoring Merit-Based Opportunity," by President Donald Trump, January 21, 2025; and Executive Order 14152: "Defending Women from Gender Ideology Extremism and Restoring Biological Truth to the Federal Government," by President Donald Trump, January 20, 2025.

4. Carol M. Swain, *The New White Nationalism in America: Its Challenge to Integration* (New York City: Cambridge University Press), p. 139.

5. "A Brief History of Affirmative Action," Office of Equal Opportunity and Diversity,"

NOTES

    https://www.oeod.uci.edu/policies/aa_history.php#:~:text=11246%20in%201965.-,Executive%20Order%2011246,receiving%20federal%20contracts%20and%20subcontracts

6   Genevieve Carlton, PhD, "A History of Affirmative Action in College Admissions," best colleges.com, updated December 7, 2022, https://www.bestcolleges.com/news/analysis/2020/08/10/history-affirmative-action-college/

7   Jane Holzka, "Philadelphia Plan," encyclopedia.com, https://www.encyclopedia.com/history/encyclopedias-almanacs-transcripts-and-maps/philadelphia-plan

8   Executive Order 14168, "Defending Women From Gender Ideology Extremism and Restoring Biological Truth to the Federal Government," by President Donald Trump, 90 Fed. Reg. 8401 (January 30, 2025).

9   John David Skrentny, *The Ironies of Affirmative Action: Politics, Culture, and Justice in America* (Chicago: University of Chicago Press, 1996).

10   National Advisory Commission on Civil Disorders, *The Kerner Report* (Princeton, NJ: Princeton University Press, 2016) p. 2.

11   U.S. Department of Labor, Glass Ceiling Commission Report (1995): "Good for Business: Making Full Use of the Nation's Human Capital: The Environmental Scan: A Fact-Finding Report of the Federal Glass Ceiling Commission." Washington, DC: U.S. Government Printing Office, 1995; Kimberlé Crenshaw, "Framing Affirmative Action," *Michigan Law Review First Impressions 105*, no. 1 (2006): 123–33. https://repository.law.umich.edu/mlr_fi/vol105/iss1/4; Tim Wise, *Affirmative Action: Racial Preference in Black and White* (New York: Routledge, 20050.

12   Frank Dobbin and Alexandra Kaley, "Why Diversity Programs Fail," *Harvard Business Review,* July-August 2016, https://hbr.org/2016/07/why-diversity-programs-fail

13   Michael Levensen, "Jury Awards $10 Million to White Male Executive in Discrimination Case," *New York Times,* October 28, 2021, https://www.nytimes.com/2021/10/28/us/david-duvall-firing-lawsuit-diversity.html

14   Levensen, "Jury Awards $10 Million to White Male Executive in Discrimination Case."

15   Levensen.

16   Hannah Grossman, "Trans Swimmer Lia Thomas Photographed Wearing 'Disturbing' Antifa Shirt: 'Doesn't This Make So Much Sense?,'" FoxNews,

July 19, 2023, https://www.foxnews.com/media/trans-swimmer-lia-thomas-photographed-wearing-disturbing-antifa-shirt-doesnt-this-make-sense

17 Executive order 14201, "Keeping Men Out of Women's Sports," President Donald Trump, https://www.whitehouse.gov/presidential-actions/2025/02/keeping-men-out-of-womens-sports/, February 5, 2025.

18 Olivia Land, "Two Kappa Kappa Gamma Alumni Ousted After Backing Lawsuit to Remove Transgender Member," *New York Post*, November 14, 2023, https://nypost.com/2023/11/14/news/longtime-kappa-kappa-gamma-members-ousted-over-wyoming-lawsuit/

19 White House, "Press Briefing by Press Secretary Karine Jean-Pierre and the Cast of 'The L Word' and 'The L Word: Generation Q,' " April 25, 2023, https://www.whitehouse.gov/briefing-room/press-briefings/2023/04/25/press-briefing-by-press-secretary-karine-jean-pierre-and-the-cast-of-the-l-word-and-the-l-word-generation-q/#:~:text=Today%20I'm%20honored%20to,funny%2C%20and%20resilient%20queer%20women

20 Stephanie Saul, "If Affirmative Action Ends. College Admissions May Be Changed Forever," *New York Times*, updated January 26, 2023.

21 Sana Pashankar, "If Affirmative Action is Overturned, How Could It Change Duke Admissions?" *The Chronicle*, Duke University, February 13, 2023.

22 Hilary Burns, "Meet Edward Blum, the Man Behind the Harvard Affirmative Action Case," *Boston Globe,* May 29, 2023, www.bostonglobe.com/2023/05/29/metro/harvard-affirmative-action-case-meet-ed-blum/?p1=Article_Recirc_Most_Popular&p1=Article_Recirc_Most_Popular

23 Hilary Burns, "Meet Edward Blum, the Man Behind the Harvard Affirmative Action Case," *Boston Globe.*

24 Burns, "Meet Edward Blum, the Man Behind the Harvard Affirmative Action Case."

25 Burns.

26 Stephanie Saul, "If Affirmative Action Ends, College Admissions May Be Changed Forever," *New York Times*, updated January 26, 2023.

27 Saul, "If Affirmative Action Ends, College Admissions May Be Changed Forever."

28 Morrison Foerster Law Firm, "Are Workplace Diversity Programs in Jeopardy if the Supreme Court Ends Affirmative Action in College Admissions?" March 29, 2023, https://www.mofo.com/resources/insights/230329-are-workplace-diversity-programs-in-jeopardy

29 Erin Kelly and Frank Dobbin, "How Affirmative Action Became Diversity Management: Employer Response to Antidiscrimination Law, 1961 to 1996," *American Behavioral Scientist*, April 1998, https://scholar.harvard.edu/dobbin/publications/how-affirmative-action-became-diversity-managementemployer-response-antidiscrimi

30 Kelly and Dobbin.

31 Genevieve Carlton, PhD, "A History of Affirmative Action in College Admissions," best colleges.com, updated December 7, 2022, https://www.bestcolleges.com/news/analysis/2020/08/10/history-affirmative-action-college/

32 Derrick A. Bell, *Race, Racism and American Law* (Boston: Little Brown, 6th ed., 2008)

Chapter 2

1 Carol M. Swain, *The New White Nationalism in America: Its Challenge to Integration* (Cambridge, UK: Cambridge University Press, 2002), p. 156, from Richardson, Messages and Papers of the Presidents, Vol. 2, pp. 398-405, cited in Albert P. Blaustein, *Civil Rights and the American Negro* (New York: Washington Square Press, 1969).

2 "Most Black Students at Harvard Are From High-Income Families," *Journal of Blacks in America*, 2004, https://www.jbhe.com/news_views/52_harvard-blackstudents.html

3 Carol M. Swain, *Black Faces, Black Interests: The Representation of African Americans in Congress* (Boston: Harvard University Press, 1993, 1996).

4 Roger E. Hernandez, "Skirting the Real Issue—Racism," *Washington Post*, February 10, 1995, https://www.washingtonpost.com/archive/opinions/1995/02/10/skirting-the-real-issue-racism/1f3aba94-6da6-4845-99f6-ed6b1a914cdb/

5 Adam Tanner, "Why a Racial Remark at Rutgers University Stirs Such Emotion," *Christian Science Monitor*, February 13, 1995, https://www.csmonitor.com/1995/0213/13031.html

6 Alex Oliveira, "Virginia School Chief Denies National Merit Awards Were Withheld Due to 'Equity' Amid Claims 17 High Schools Delayed Handing Out Accolades to Avoid Hurting Other Students' Feelings," DailyMail.com, January 25, 2023, https://www.dailymail.co.uk/news/article-11676761/Virginia-school-chief-denies-National-Merit-Awards-withheld-equity.html

7 Maggie Severns, "Woman Who Killed Affirmative Action," *Politico*, April 24, 2014, https://www.politico.com/story/2014/04/jennifer-gratz-affirmative-action-michigan-105913

Notes

8   Richard H. Sander and Stuart Taylor Jr., *Mismatch: How Affirmative Action Hurts Students It's Intended to Help, and Why Universities Won't Admit It* (New York: Basic Books, 2012) p. 368.

9   Roland Fryer, "Build Freer Schools and Make Yale and Harvard Fund Them," *New York Times*, July 5, 2023, https://www.nytimes.com/interactive/2023/07/05/opinion/affirmative-action-college-admissions.html

Chapter 3

1   President Barack Obama, "Executive Order on Diversity, Equity, Inclusion, and Accessibility in the Federal Workforce," The White House, June 25, 2021, https://www.whitehouse.gov/briefing-room/presidential-actions/2021/06/25/executive-order-on-diversity-equity-inclusion-and-accessibility-in-the-federal-workforce/

2   Obama, "Executive Order on Diversity, Equity, Inclusion, and Accessibility in the Federal Workforce."

3   Obama.

4   Aja Romano, "Google Has Fired the Engineer Whose Anti-Diversity Memo Reflects a Divided Tech Culture," vox.com, August 8, 2017, https://www.vox.com/identities/2017/8/8/16106728/google-fired-engineer-anti-diversity-memo

5   Romano, "Google Has Fired the Engineer Whose Anti-Diversity Memo Reflects a Divided Tech Culture."

6   Romano.

7   Associated Press, "Mozilla CEO Resignation Raises Free-Speech Issues," as it appeared in *USA Today*, April 4, 2014, https://www.usatoday.com/story/news/nation/2014/04/04/mozilla-ceo-resignation-free-speech/7328759/

8   Associated Press, "Mozilla CEO Resignation Raises Free-Speech Issues."

9   "Mozilla CEO Resignation Raises Free-Speech Issues."

10 Rohini Anand and Mary-Frances Winters, "A Retrospective View of Corporate Diversity Training from 1964 to the Present," *Academy of Management Learning & Education*, September 2008, pp. 356-372, https://journals.aom.org/doi/abs/10.5465/amle.2008.34251673

11 Anand and Winters, "A Retrospective View of Corporate Diversity Training from 1964 to the Present."

12 Anand and Winters.

13 Anand and Winters.

Notes

14. Jonathan Turley, " 'What's More Tragic Is Capitalism': BLM Faces Bankruptcy as Founder Cullors Is Cut by Warner Bros.," jonathanturley,org, May 28, 2023, https://jonathanturley.org/2023/05/28/the-stuff-that-dreams-are-made-of-blm-faces-bankruptcy-as-founder-cullors-is-cut-by-warner-bros/
15. Turley, " 'What's More Tragic Is Capitalism': BLM Faces Bankruptcy as Founder Cullors Is Cut by Warner Bros."
16. Turley.
17. Turley.

Chapter 4

1. Rahm Emanuel, "Let's Make Sure This Crisis Doesn't Go to Waste," *Washington Post*, March 25, 2020, https://www.washingtonpost.com/opinions/2020/03/25/lets-make-sure-this-crisis-doesnt-go-waste/, viewed June 11, 2023.
2. Paolo Gaudiano, "Two Years After George Floyd's Murder, Is Your DEI Strategy Performative or Sustainable," *Forbes*, June 27, 2022, https://www.forbes.com/sites/paologaudiano/2022/06/27/two-years-after-george-floyd-is-your-dei-strategy-performative-or-sustainable/?sh=39db300c6aaa, viewed June 18, 2023.
3. https://www.documentcloud.org/documents/6936176-Autopsy-2020-3700-Floyd, viewed June 18, 2023.
4. Erin Donaghue, "Two Autopsies Both Find George Floyd Died by Homicide, But Differ on Some Key Details," CBS News, June 4, 2020, https://www.cbsnews.com/news/george-floyd-death-autopsies-homicide-axphyxiation-details/, viewed June 18, 2023.
5. Rahm Emanuel, "Let's Make Sure This Crisis Doesn't Go to Waste."
6. *New York Times*, "How George Floyd Died, and What Happened Next," July 29, 2022, https://www.nytimes.com/article/george-floyd.html, viewed June 14, 2023.
7. Christopher F. Rufo, "When 'Diversity Training' Is All About Feeding Racism," *New York Post*, July 10, 2020, https://manhattan.institute/article/when-diversity-training-is-all-about-feeding-racism
8. Rufo, "When 'Diversity Training' Is All About Feeding Racism."
9. Danielle Wiener-Bronner and Kristina Sgueglia, "Starbucks Says It Fired Her for an 'Absence of Leadership.' She Says It Was Because of Her Race. A Jury Returned a $25.6 Million Verdict in Her Favor," CNN, June 14,

2023, https://www.cnn.com/2023/06/14/business/starbucks-manager-racial-discrimination/index.html, viewed June 15, 2023.

10 Danielle Wiener-Bronner and Kristina Sgueglia, "Starbucks Says It Fired Her for an 'Absence of Leadership.' "

11 Heather Haddon, "Starbucks Closing Some Stores, Citing Safety Concerns in Certain Cafes," *Wall Street Journal,* July 12, 2022, https://www.wsj.com/articles/starbucks-closing-some-stores-citing-safety-concerns-in-certain-cafes-11657588871, viewed June 15, 2023.

12 Sarah Rumpf-Whitten, "University of Minnesota Faces Backlash over Summer Research Program Restricted to Nonwhite Students," Fox News, May 21, 2023, https://www.foxnews.com/us/university-minnesota-faces-backlash-over-summer-research-pr

13 Cole Premo, "University of Minnesota Among Dozens of Schools Under Federal Investigation for Allegations of Racial Discrimination," WCCO News, March 14, 2025, https://www.cbsnews.com/minnesota/news/university-of-minnesota-department-of-education-investigation-allegations-racial-discrimination/

14 Rumpf-Whitten, "University of Minnesota Face Backlash over Summer Research Program Restricted to Nonwhite Students."

15 Dana Kennedy, "Inside the CEI System Pushing Brands to Endorse Celebs Like Dylan Mulvaney," *New York Post,* April 7, 2023, https://nypost.com/2023/04/07/inside-the-woke-scoring-system-guiding-american-companies/

16 Dana Kennedy, "Inside the CEI System Pushing Brands to Endorse Celebs Like Dylan Mulvaney."

17 Kennedy.

18 Kennedy.

19 Kennedy.

20 Cortney O'Brien, "Court Rules Against Employee Fired for Refusing to Attend LGBTQ Training Session," Fox News, March 15, 2023, https://www.foxnews.com/media/court-rules-against-employee-fired-refusing-attend-lgbtq-training-session

21 Charlotte Allen, "The DEI Invasion: Ideological Creep in Law and Medicine," *Epoch Times,* May 24, 2023, https://www.theepochtimes.com/the-dei-invasion-ideological-creep-in-law-and-medicine_5284040.html

22 Charlotte Allen, "The DEI Invasion: Ideological Creep in Law and Medicine."

NOTES

23 Human Rights Campaign, "HRC Foundation Announces CEI Score Deductions for Companies Retreating from LGBTQ+ Commitments," HRC.org, September 17, 2024, https://www.hrc.org/press-releases/hrc-foundation-announces-cei-score-deductions

24 Tractor Supply Company, "Statement on Corporate Responsibility Priorities," TSC.com, June 27, 2024, https://www.tractorsupply.com/tsc/cms/company-statement-2024; Joe Schoffstall, "Target's LGBTQ+ Push Backfires, Stock Plummets Amid Boycotts," FoxBusiness.com, August 23, 2023, https://www.foxbusiness.com/retail/targets-lgbtq-push-backfires; Martin Armstrong, "DEI and ESG Mentions in Earnings Calls Drop 31% as Companies Pivot," ArmstrongEconomics.com, September 5, 2023, https://www.armstrongeconomics.com/business/dei-esg-decline-2023

25 Robby Starbuck, "Why Companies Are Dropping DEI: A Win for Common Sense," X.com, October 15, 2024, https://x.com/robbystarbuck/status/184620123456789.

26 Human Rights Campaign Foundation, "Corporate Equality Index 2025: Rating Workplaces on Lesbian, Gay, Bisexual, Transgender and Queer Equality," Reports.hrc.org, January 6, 2025, https://reports.hrc.org/corporate-equality-index-2025

27 Nadine El-Bawab and Melissa Repko, "One Year After George Floyd's Death: 6 Reflections on Corporate America's Progress," CNBC, May 26, 2021, https://www.cnbc.com/2021/05/26/one-year-after-george-floyds-death-6-reflections-on-corporate-americas-progress.html

Chapter 5

1 James A. Lindsay, "The Marxist Roots of DEI Workshop: Session 2—Diversity," New Discourses video presentation, April 4, 2023, https://newdiscourses.com/2023/04/marxist-roots-of-dei-workshop-all-sessions/

2 Jathon Sapsford, "Republican Attorneys General Warn Top U.S. Businesses over 'Discrimination,'" *Wall Street Journal,* July 14, 2023, https://www.wsj.com/articles/republican-attorneys-general-warn-top-u-s-businesses-over-discrimination-1eb78d29

3 Darlene McCormick Sanchez, "UT Austin Spends over $13 million on Diversity, Equity, and Inclusion Salaries: Documents," *Epoch Times,* May 20, 2023, https://www.theepochtimes.com/ut-austin-spends-over-13-million-on-diversity-equity-and-inclusion-salaries-documents_5280452.html,

4 Darlene McCormick Sanchez, "UT Austin Spends over $13 million on Diversity, Equity, and Inclusion Salaries: Documents."

Notes

5   McCormick Sanchez.

6   Sherry Sylvester, "Texas War to End DEI is Just Beginning," Cannononlline.com, July 5, 2023, https://thecannononline.com/texas-war-to-end-dei-is-just-beginning/

7   Olivia Land, "Former Penn State Professor Zack DePiero Claims College Said English Language Is 'Racist,'" *New York Post*, June 26, 2023, www.msn.com/en-us/news/us/former-penn-state-professor-zack-de-piero-claims-college-said-english-language-is-racist/ar-AA1d7yRn,

8   Land, "Former Penn State Professor Zack DePiero Claims College Said English Language Is 'Racist.'"

9   https://www.linkedin.com/showcase/hr-dive-human-resources-and-workforce-management-news/

10   Laura Kalser, "Some DEI Policies Send the Wrong Message, Survey Warns," *HR Dive*, November 16, 2022, https://www.hrdive.com/news/dei-policies-reverse-discrimination/636561/

11   Jonathan Turley, "Chicago-Area Teacher Sues After Being Fired for Criticism of Protests After George Floyd Murder," jonathanturley.org, July 26, 2021, https://jonathanturley.org/2021/07/26/chicago-area-teacher/Chicago-Area Teacher Sues After Being Fired For Criticism Of Protests After George Floyd Murder

12   Kenneth R. Timmerman, *Shakedown: Exposing the Real Jesse Jackson* (Washington, DC: Regnery, 2012).

13   Turley, "Chicago-Area Teacher Sues After Being Fired for Criticism of Protests After George Floyd Murder."

14   Timmerman, *Shakedown: Exposing the Real Jesse Jackson*.

15   Zachary Faria, "The NFL Meets with Race-Baiter Al Sharpton to Discuss Racial Quotas," *Washington Examiner*, February 9, 2022, https://www.washingtonexaminer.com/opinion/the-nfl-meets-with-race-baiter-al-sharpton-to-discuss-racial-quotas, viewed July 12, 2023.

16   Khorri Atkinson, "Corporate Diversity Pledges Fizzle Amid Layoffs, GOP Backlash," news.bloomberglaw.com, March 9, 2023, https://news.bloomberglaw.com/daily-labor-report/corporate-diversity-pledges-fizzle-amid-layoffs-gop-backlash

17   Kelsey Minor, "Three Years After George Floyd's Murder: Where Is DEI Now, and What Have Companies Learned?" *Senior Executive*, February 10, 2023, https://seniorexecutive.com/three-years-after-george-floyds-murder-where-is-dei-now-and-what-have-companies-learned/#:~:text=The%20result%20of%20the%20company's,includes%20equity%20pay%20and%20promotions

18   Jonathan Turley, " 'What's More Tragic Is Capitalism': BLM Faces Bankruptcy as Founder Cullors Is Cut by Warner Bros.," jonathanturley.org, May 28, 2023, https://jonathanturley.org/2023/05/28/the-stuff-that-dreams-are-made-of-blm-faces-bankruptcy-as-founder-cullors-is-cut-by-warner-bros/

19   Morrison Foerster Law Firm, "Are Workplace Diversity Programs in Jeopardy if the Supreme Court Ends Affirmative Action in College Admissions?" March 29, 2023, https://www.mofo.com/resources/insights/230329-are-workplace-diversity-programs-in-jeopardy

20   Erika Johnson, "Top 4 Reasons Diversity and Inclusion Programs Fail," *Forbes*, March 29, 2021, https://www.forbes.com/sites/forbeseq/2021/03/29/top-4-reasons-diversity-and-inclusion-programs-fail/

21   Frank Dobbin and Alexandra Kalev, "Spotlight on Building a Diverse Organization: Why Diversity Programs Fail," *Harvard Business Review*, July-August 2016, https://hbr.org/2016/07/why-diversity-programs-fail, viewed June 15, 2023.

22   Dobbin and Kalev, "Spotlight on Building a Diverse Organization: Why Diversity Programs Fail."

Chapter 6

1   U.S. Supreme Court Chief Justice John Roberts, Majority Opinion, *Students for Fair Admissions v. President and Fellows of Harvard College*, https://supreme.justia.com/cases/federal/us/600/20-1199/#tab-opinion-4758916

2   U.S. Supreme Court Justice Clarence Thomas, Concurring Opinion, *Students for Fair Admissions v. President and Fellows of Harvard College*. https://supreme.justia.com/cases/federal/us/600/20-1199/

3   Deborah White, "Barack Obama's Inspiring 2004 Democratic Convention Speech," thoughtco.com, October 16, 2017, www.thoughtco.com/obama-speech-2004-democratic-convention-3325333,

4   Carol M. Swain, "Is America Ready for a Black President? America is Ready, But It Won't Be A Veteran of the Civil Rights Movement," *Ebony* 62, no. 3 (January 2007) p. 141, as quoted in Carol M. Swain, "Racial Politics, President Obama and Me," Ch. 7, *Be the People: A Call to Reclaim America's Faith and Promise* (Nashville, Thomas Nelson Press, 2011), p. 191.

5.   Robert O'Harrow Jr., "Videos Show Closed-Door Sessions of Leading Conservative Activists: 'Be Not Afraid of the Accusations That You're a Voter

Notes

Suppressor,'" *Washington Post*, October 14, 2020, https://www.washingtonpost.com/investigations/council-national-policy-video/2020/10/14/367f24c2-f793-11ea-a510-f57d8ce76e11_story.html

6. Te-Ping Chen and Ray A. Smith, "No One Is Happy about Diversity Efforts at Work," *Wall Street Journal*, July 3, 2023, https://www.wsj.com/articles/diversity-workplace-affirmative-action-dei-3646683b, viewed July 9, 2023.

7. Chen and Smith, "No One Is Happy about Diversity Efforts at Work," *Wall Street Journal*, July 3, 2023.

8. Stephen R. Covey, T*he Seven Habits of Highly Effective People: Restoring the Character Ethic* (New York, Simon and Schuster, 1989).

9. Peter Lencioni, *The Five Dysfunctions of a Team* (London: Jossey-Bass, 2002).

10. Carol M. Swain, *The New White Nationalism in America: Its Challenge to Integration* (New York: Cambridge University Press, 2002).

11. Richard Sander and Stuart Taylor Jr., *Mismatch: How Affirmative Action Hurts Students It's Intended to Help, and Why Universities Won't Admit It* (New York: Basic Books, 2012).

12. Amazon book summary, *Mismatch: How Affirmative Action Hurts Students It's Intended to Help, and Why Universities Won't Admit It*, by Richard Sander and Stuart Taylor Jr., https://www.amazon.com/Mismatch-Affirmative-Students-%C2%92s-Universities/dp/0465029965/ref=sr_1_11?crid=3N3B4WC82DYM2&keywords=richard+sanders&qid=1689092071&s=books&sprefix=richard+sanders%2Cstripbooks%2C192&sr=1-11

13. WorldBlu, business management company, https://www.worldblu.com

14. Mike Hardwick, Churchill Mortgage Corporation, interview with Carol Swain, October 26, 2022.

15. "A Plan to Make 'Diversity, Equity, And Inclusion' Die," *The Federalist*, October 28, 2022, https://unitytrainingsolutions.com/a-plan-to-make-diversity-equity-and-inclusion-die/

Epilogue

1. Nicquel Terry Ellis, "What Is DEI, and Why Is It Dividing America?", cnn.com, January 23, 2025, https://www.cnn.com/2025/01/22/us/dei-diversity-equity-inclusion-explained/index.html

2. Alicia Gonzales, "Attacks on DEI Initiatives Are Fueling A Resignation Crisis," forbes.com, January 26, 2024, https://www.forbes.com/sites/aliciagonzalez/2024/01/26/attacks-on-dei-initiatives-are-fueling-a-resignation-crisis/ ; "Which U.S. Companies Are Pulling Back on Diversity Initiatives." AP News, March 7, 2025, https://apnews.com/article/dei-diversity-equity-inclusion-companies-lawsuits-

NOTES

2193ef0a864db968e6934f971f78e8f2

3   Kate Gibson, Emmet Lyons, "Meta Ends Diversity Programs, Joining McDonald's, Walmart and Other Major Companies to Back Off DEI," January 16, 2025, https://www.cbsnews.com/news/meta-dei-programs-mcdonalds-walmart-ford-diversity/

4   "Ending Radical and Wasteful Government DEI Programs and Preferencing," the White House," January 20, 2025, https://www.whitehouse.gov/presidential-actions/2025/01/ending-radical-and-wasteful-government-dei-programs-and-preferencing/

5   Elizabeth Dorminey, "Bye Bye, DEI: President Trump Issues Executive Order Revoking Biden's Diversity, Equity, and Inclusion Rules and Axing Affirmative Action," The Federalist Society, January 27, 2025, https://fedsoc.org/commentary/fedsoc-blog/bye-bye-dei-president-trump-issues-executive-order-revoking-biden-s-diversity-equity-and-inclusion-rules-and-axing-affirmative-action

6   Dorminey, "Bye Bye, DEI: President Trump Issues Executive Order Revoking Biden's Diversity, Equity, and Inclusion Rules and Axing Affirmative Action."

7   Tina Opie and Ella F. Washington, "Why Companies Can — and Should — Recommit to DEI in the Wake of the SCOTUS Decision," Harvard Business Review, July 27, 2023, https://hbr.org/2023/07/why-companies-can-and-should-recommit-to-dei-in-the-wake-of-the-scotus-decision

8   Miranda Jeyaretnam, "These U.S. Companies Are Not Ditching DEI Amid Trump's Crackdown," *Time*, February 26, 2025, https://time.com/7261857/us-companies-keep-dei-initiatives-list-trump-diversity-order-crackdown/

9   Kiara Alfonseca, "A Look at What DEI Means Amid Trump Executive Orders," ABC News. January 24, 2025, https://abcnews.go.com/US/dei-programs/story?id=97004455

10 Alfonseca, "A Look at What DEI Means Amid Trump Executive Orders."

APPENDIX A

President Donald Trump's January 2025 Executive Orders for Diversity, Equity, and Inclusion (DEI)

ON JANUARY 20 AND 21, 2025, PRESIDENT DONALD J. TRUMP issued a series of executive orders aimed at dismantling Diversity, Equity, and Inclusion (DEI) initiatives and affirmative action requirements within the federal government and its contractors. These orders reflect a policy shift toward merit-based systems and the elimination of what the administration deems "illegal discrimination" under the guise of DEI programs. Below are the key orders, their texts, and brief descriptions.

(1) Executive Order 14151, Ending Radical and Wasteful Government DEI Programs and Preferencing[1]

By the authority vested in me as President by the Constitution and the laws of the United States of America, it is hereby ordered:

Section 1. Purpose and Policy. The Biden Administration forced illegal and immoral discrimination programs, going by the name "diversity, equity, and inclusion" (DEI), into virtually all aspects of the Federal Government, in areas ranging from airline safety to the military. This was a concerted effort stemming from President Biden's first day in office, when he issued Executive Order 13985, "Advancing Racial Equity and Support for Underserved Communities Through the Federal Government."

Pursuant to Executive Order 13985 and follow-on orders, nearly every Federal agency and entity submitted "Equity Action Plans" to detail the ways that they have furthered DEIs infiltration of the Federal Government. The public release of these plans demonstrated immense public waste and shameful discrimination. That ends today. Americans deserve a government committed to serving every person with equal dignity and respect, and to expending precious taxpayer resources only on making America great.

Sec. 2. Implementation. (a) The Director of the Office of Management and Budget (OMB), assisted by the Attorney General and the Director of the Office of Personnel Management (OPM), shall coordinate the termination of all discriminatory programs, including illegal DEI and "diversity, equity, inclusion, and accessibility" (DEIA) mandates, policies, programs, preferences, and activities in the Federal Government, under whatever name they appear. To carry out this directive, the Director of OPM, with the assistance of the Attorney General as requested, shall review and revise, as appropriate, all existing Federal employment practices, union contracts, and training policies or programs to comply with this order. Federal employment practices, including Federal employee performance reviews, shall reward individual initiative, skills, performance, and hard work and shall not under any circumstances consider DEI or DEIA factors, goals, policies, mandates, or requirements.

(b) Each agency, department, or commission head, in consultation with the Attorney General, the Director of OMB, and the Director of OPM, as appropriate, shall take the following actions within sixty days of this order:

(i) terminate, to the maximum extent allowed by law, all DEI, DEIA, and "environmental justice" offices and positions (including but not limited to "Chief Diversity Officer" positions); all "equity action plans," "equity" actions, initiatives, or programs, "equity-related" grants or contracts; and all DEI or DEIA performance requirements for employees, contractors, or grantees.

(ii) provide the Director of the OMB with a list of all:

(A) agency or department DEI, DEIA, or "environmental justice" positions, committees, programs, services, activities, budgets, and expenditures in existence on November 4, 2024, and an assessment of whether these positions, committees, programs, services, activities, budgets, and expenditures have been misleadingly relabeled in an attempt to preserve their pre-November 4, 2024 function;

Appendix A: President Trump's January 2025 EOs for DEI

(B) Federal contractors who have provided DEI training or DEI training materials to agency or department employees; and

(C) Federal grantees who received Federal funding to provide or advance DEI, DEIA, or "environmental justice" programs, services, or activities since January 20, 2021.

(iii) direct the deputy agency or department head to:

(A) assess the operational impact (e.g., the number of new DEI hires) and cost of the prior administration's DEI, DEIA, and "environmental justice" programs and policies; and

(B) recommend actions, such as Congressional notifications under 28 U.S.C. 530D, to align agency or department programs, activities, policies, regulations, guidance, employment practices, enforcement activities, contracts (including set-asides), grants, consent orders, and litigating positions with the policy of equal dignity and respect identified in section 1 of this order. The agency or department head and the Director of OMB shall jointly ensure that the deputy agency or department head has the authority and resources needed to carry out this directive.

(c) To inform and advise the President, so that he may formulate appropriate and effective civil-rights policies for the Executive Branch, the Assistant to the President for Domestic Policy shall convene a monthly meeting attended by the Director of OMB, the Director of OPM, and each deputy agency or department head to:

(i) hear reports on the prevalence and the economic and social costs of DEI, DEIA, and "environmental justice" in agency or department programs, activities, policies, regulations, guidance, employment practices, enforcement activities, contracts (including set-asides), grants, consent orders, and litigating positions;

(ii) discuss any barriers to measures to comply with this order; and

(iii) monitor and track agency and department progress and identify potential areas for additional Presidential or legislative action to advance the policy of equal dignity and respect.

Sec. 3. Severability. If any provision of this order, or the application of any provision to any person or circumstance, is held to be invalid, the remainder of this order and the application of its provisions to any other persons or circumstances shall not be affected.

Sec. 4. General Provisions. (a) Nothing in this order shall be construed to impair or otherwise affect:

(i) the authority granted by law to an executive department or agency, or the head thereof; or

(ii) the functions of the Director of the Office of Management and Budget relating to budgetary, administrative, or legislative proposals.

(b) This order shall be implemented consistent with applicable law and subject to the availability of appropriations.

(c) This order is not intended to, and does not, create any right or benefit, substantive or procedural, enforceable at law or in equity by any party against the United States, its departments, agencies, or entities, its officers, employees, or agents, or any other person.

(2) Executive Order 14168: Defending Women from Gender Ideology Extremism and Restoring Biological Truth to the Federal Government[2]

By the authority vested in me as President by the Constitution and the laws of the United States of America, including section 7301 of title 5, United States Code, it is hereby ordered:

Section 1. Purpose. Across the country, ideologues who deny the biological reality of sex have increasingly used legal and other socially coercive means to permit men to self-identify as women and gain access to intimate single-sex spaces and activities designed for women, from women's domestic abuse shelters to women's workplace showers. This is wrong. Efforts to eradicate the biological reality of sex fundamentally attack women by depriving them of their dignity, safety, and well-being. The erasure of sex in language and policy has a corrosive impact not just on women but on the validity of the entire American system. Basing Federal policy on truth is critical to scientific inquiry, public safety, morale, and trust in government itself.

This unhealthy road is paved by an ongoing and purposeful attack against the ordinary and longstanding use and understanding of biological and scientific terms, replacing the immutable biological reality of sex with an internal, fluid, and subjective sense of self unmoored from biological facts. Invalidating the true and biological category of "woman" improperly transforms laws and policies designed to protect sex-based opportunities into laws and policies that undermine them, replacing longstanding, cherished legal rights and values with an identity-based, inchoate social concept.

Accordingly, my Administration will defend women's rights and protect freedom of conscience by using clear and accurate language and policies that recognize women are biologically female, and men are biologically male.

Sec. 2. Policy and Definitions. It is the policy of the United States to recognize two sexes, male and female. These sexes are not changeable and are grounded in fundamental and incontrovertible reality. Under my direction, the Executive Branch will enforce all sex-protective laws to promote this reality, and the following definitions shall govern all Executive interpretation of and application of Federal law and administration policy:

(a) "Sex" shall refer to an individual's immutable biological classification as either male or female. "Sex" is not a synonym for and does not include the concept of "gender identity."

(b) "Women" or "woman" and "girls" or "girl" shall mean adult and juvenile human females, respectively.

(c) "Men" or "man" and "boys" or "boy" shall mean adult and juvenile human males, respectively.

(d) "Female" means a person belonging, at conception, to the sex that produces the large reproductive cell.

(e) "Male" means a person belonging, at conception, to the sex that produces the small reproductive cell.

(f) "Gender ideology" replaces the biological category of sex with an ever-shifting concept of self-assessed gender identity, permitting the false claim that males can identify as and thus become women and vice versa, and requiring all institutions of society to regard this false claim as true. Gender ideology includes the idea that there is a vast spectrum of genders that are disconnected from one's sex. Gender ideology is internally inconsistent, in that it diminishes sex as an identifiable or useful category but nevertheless maintains that it is possible for a person to be born in the wrong sexed body.

Appendix A: President Trump's January 2025 EOs for DEI

(g) "Gender identity" reflects a fully internal and subjective sense of self, disconnected from biological reality and sex and existing on an infinite continuum, that does not provide a meaningful basis for identification and cannot be recognized as a replacement for sex.

Sec. 3. Recognizing Women Are Biologically Distinct From Men. (a) Within 30 days of the date of this order, the Secretary of Health and Human Services shall provide to the U.S. Government, external partners, and the public clear guidance expanding on the sex-based definitions set forth in this order.

(b) Each agency and all Federal employees shall enforce laws governing sex-based rights, protections, opportunities, and accommodations to protect men and women as biologically distinct sexes. Each agency should therefore give the terms "sex", "male", "female", "men", "women", "boys" and "girls" the meanings set forth in section 2 of this order when interpreting or applying statutes, regulations, or guidance and in all other official agency business, documents, and communications.

(c) When administering or enforcing sex-based distinctions, every agency and all Federal employees acting in an official capacity on behalf of their agency shall use the term "sex" and not "gender" in all applicable Federal policies and documents.

(d) The Secretaries of State and Homeland Security, and the Director of the Office of Personnel Management, shall implement changes to require that government-issued identification documents, including passports, visas, and Global Entry cards, accurately reflect the holder's sex, as defined under section 2 of this order; and the Director of the Office of Personnel Management shall ensure that applicable personnel records accurately report Federal employees' sex, as defined by section 2 of this order.

(e) Agencies shall remove all statements, policies, regulations, forms, communications, or other internal and external messages that promote or otherwise inculcate gender ideology, and shall cease issuing such statements, policies, regulations, forms, communications or other messages. Agency forms that require an individual's sex shall list male or female, and shall not request gender identity. Agencies shall take all necessary steps, as permitted by law, to end the Federal funding of gender ideology.

(f) The prior Administration argued that the Supreme Court's decision in *Bostock v. Clayton County* (2020), which addressed Title VII of

Appendix A: President Trump's January 2025 EOs for DEI

the Civil Rights Act of 1964, requires gender identity-based access to single-sex spaces under, for example, Title IX of the Educational Amendments Act. This position is legally untenable and has harmed women. The Attorney General shall therefore immediately issue guidance to agencies to correct the misapplication of the Supreme Court's decision in *Bostock v. Clayton County* (2020) to sex-based distinctions in agency activities. In addition, the Attorney General shall issue guidance and assist agencies in protecting sex-based distinctions, which are explicitly permitted under Constitutional and statutory precedent.

(g) Federal funds shall not be used to promote gender ideology. Each agency shall assess grant conditions and grantee preferences and ensure grant funds do not promote gender ideology.

Sec. 4. Privacy in Intimate Spaces. (a) The Attorney General and Secretary of Homeland Security shall ensure that males are not detained in women's prisons or housed in women's detention centers, including through amendment, as necessary, of Part 115.41 of title 28, Code of Federal Regulations and interpretation guidance regarding the Americans with Disabilities Act.

(b) The Secretary of Housing and Urban Development shall prepare and submit for notice and comment rulemaking a policy to rescind the final rule entitled "Equal Access in Accordance with an Individual's Gender Identity in Community Planning and Development Programs" of September 21, 2016, 81 FR 64763, and shall submit for public comment a policy protecting women seeking single-sex rape shelters.

(c) The Attorney General shall ensure that the Bureau of Prisons revises its policies concerning medical care to be consistent with this order, and shall ensure that no Federal funds are expended for any medical procedure, treatment, or drug for the purpose of conforming an inmate's appearance to that of the opposite sex.

(d) Agencies shall effectuate this policy by taking appropriate action to ensure that intimate spaces designated for women, girls, or females (or for men, boys, or males) are designated by sex and not identity.

Sec. 5. Protecting Rights. The Attorney General shall issue guidance to ensure the freedom to express the binary nature of sex and the right to single-sex spaces in workplaces and federally funded entities covered by the Civil Rights Act of 1964. In accordance with that guidance, the Attorney General, the Secretary of Labor, the General Counsel and

Appendix A: President Trump's January 2025 EOs for DEI

Chair of the Equal Employment Opportunity Commission, and each other agency head with enforcement responsibilities under the Civil Rights Act shall prioritize investigations and litigation to enforce the rights and freedoms identified.

Sec. 6. Bill Text. Within 30 days of the date of this order, the Assistant to the President for Legislative Affairs shall present to the President proposed bill text to codify the definitions in this order.

Sec. 7. Agency Implementation and Reporting. (a) Within 120 days of the date of this order, each agency head shall submit an update on implementation of this order to the President, through the Director of the Office of Management and Budget. That update shall address:

(i) changes to agency documents, including regulations, guidance, forms, and communications, made to comply with this order; and

(ii) agency-imposed requirements on federally funded entities, including contractors, to achieve the policy of this order.

(b) The requirements of this order supersede conflicting provisions in any previous Executive Orders or Presidential Memoranda, including but not limited to Executive Orders 13988 of January 20, 2021, 14004 of January 25, 2021, 14020 and 14021 of March 8, 2021, and 14075 of June 15, 2022. These Executive Orders are hereby rescinded, and the White House Gender Policy Council established by Executive Order 14020 is dissolved.

(c) Each agency head shall promptly rescind all guidance documents inconsistent with the requirements of this order or the Attorney General's guidance issued pursuant to this order, or rescind such parts of such documents that are inconsistent in such manner. Such documents include, but are not limited to:

(i) "The White House Toolkit on Transgender Equality";

(ii) the Department of Education's guidance documents including:

(A) "2024 Title IX Regulations: Pointers for Implementation" (July 2024);

(B) "U.S. Department of Education Toolkit: Creating Inclusive and Nondiscriminatory School Environments for LGBTQI+ Students";

(C) "U.S. Department of Education Supporting LGBTQI+ Youth and Families in School" (June 21, 2023);

(D) "Departamento de Educación de EE.UU. Apoyar a los jóvenes y familias LGBTQI+ en la escuela" (June 21, 2023);

Appendix A: President Trump's January 2025 EOs for DEI

(E) "Supporting Intersex Students: A Resource for Students, Families, and Educators" (October 2021);

(F) "Supporting Transgender Youth in School" (June 2021);

(G) "Letter to Educators on Title IX's 49th Anniversary" (June 23, 2021);

(H) "Confronting Anti-LGBTQI+ Harassment in Schools: A Resource for Students and Families" (June 2021);

(I) "Enforcement of Title IX of the Education Amendments of 1972 With Respect to Discrimination Based on Sexual Orientation and Gender Identity in Light of *Bostock v. Clayton County*" (June 22, 2021);

(J) "Education in a Pandemic: The Disparate Impacts of COVID-19 on America's Students" (June 9, 2021); and

(K) "Back-to-School Message for Transgender Students from the U.S. Depts of Justice, Education, and HHS" (Aug. 17, 2021);

(iii) the Attorney General's Memorandum of March 26, 2021 entitled "Application of *Bostock v. Clayton County* to Title IX of the Education Amendments of 1972"; and

(iv) the Equal Employment Opportunity Commission's "Enforcement Guidance on Harassment in the Workplace" (April 29, 2024).

Sec. 8. General Provisions. (a) Nothing in this order shall be construed to impair or otherwise affect:

(i) the authority granted by law to an executive department or agency, or the head thereof; or

(ii) the functions of the Director of the Office of Management and Budget relating to budgetary, administrative, or legislative proposals.

(b) This order shall be implemented consistent with applicable law and subject to the availability of appropriations.

(c) This order is not intended to, and does not, create any right or benefit, substantive or procedural, enforceable at law or in equity by any party against the United States, its departments, agencies, or entities, its officers, employees, or agents, or any other person.

(d) If any provision of this order, or the application of any provision to any person or circumstance, is held to be invalid, the remainder of this order and the application of its provisions to any other persons or circumstances shall not be affected thereby.

(3) Executive Order 14173: Ending Illegal Discrimination and Restoring Merit-Based Opportunity[3]

By the authority vested in me as President by the Constitution and the laws of the United States of America, it is hereby ordered as follows:

Section 1. Purpose.

Longstanding Federal civil-rights laws protect individual Americans from discrimination based on race, color, religion, sex, or national origin. These civil-rights protections serve as a bedrock supporting equality of opportunity for all Americans. As President, I have a solemn duty to ensure that these laws are enforced for the benefit of all Americans. Unfortunately, employers across industries, including the Federal Government itself, and other institutions such as colleges and universities, have adopted and actively use dangerous, demeaning, and immoral race- and sex-based preferences under the guise of so-called "diversity, equity, and inclusion" (DEI) or "diversity, equity, inclusion, and accessibility" (DEIA). Not only do these policies and practices violate the text and spirit of our longstanding Federal civil-rights laws, they also undermine our national unity, as they deny, discredit, and undermine the traditional American values of hard work, excellence, and individual achievement in favor of an unlawful, corrosive, and pernicious identity-based spoils system. It is the policy of the United States to protect the civil rights of all Americans and to promote individual initiative, excellence, and hard work. I therefore order all executive departments and agencies (agencies) to terminate all discriminatory and illegal preferences, mandates, policies, programs, activities, guidance, regulations, enforcement actions, consent orders, and requirements.

Section 2. Revocation.

(a) The following executive actions are hereby revoked:

(i) Executive Order 12898 of February 11, 1994 (Federal Actions to Address Environmental Justice in Minority Populations and Low-Income Populations);(ii) Executive Order 13583 of August 18, 2011 (Establishing a Coordinated Government-wide Initiative to Promote Diversity and Inclusion in the Federal Workforce);

(iii) Executive Order 13672 of July 21, 2014 (Further Amendments to Executive Order 11478, Equal Employment Opportunity in the Fed-

Appendix A: President Trump's January 2025 EOs for DEI

eral Government, and Executive Order 11246, Equal Employment Opportunity); and

(iv) The Presidential Memorandum of October 5, 2016 (Promoting Diversity and Inclusion in the National Security Workforce).

(b) The Federal contracting process shall be streamlined to enhance speed and efficiency, reduce costs, and require Federal contractors and subcontractors to comply with our civil-rights laws. Accordingly:

(i) Executive Order 11246 of September 24, 1965 (Equal Employment Opportunity), is hereby revoked. For 90 days from the date of this order, Federal contractors may continue to comply with the regulatory scheme in effect on January 20, 2025.

(ii) The Office of Federal Contract Compliance Programs within the Department of Labor shall immediately cease:

(A) Promoting "diversity";

(B) Holding Federal contractors and subcontractors responsible for taking "affirmative action"; and

(C) Allowing or encouraging Federal contractors and subcontractors to engage in workforce balancing based on race, color, sex, sexual preference, religion, or national origin.

Section 3. Terminating Illegal Discrimination in the Federal Government.

(a) The Director of the Office of Management and Budget, in consultation with the Attorney General, shall review and revise, as appropriate, all government-wide processes, directives, and guidance issued by the Office of Management and Budget to:

(i) Remove all references to DEI or DEIA principles from Federal acquisition, contracting, grants, and financial assistance procedures; and

(ii) Terminate all DEI-related mandates, requirements, programs, or activities.

(b) The head of each agency shall terminate all DEI or DEIA mandates, policies, programs, or activities within such agency.

Section 4. Ensuring Compliance with Students for Fair Admissions Decision.

Appendix A: President Trump's January 2025 EOs for DEI

Within 120 days of the date of this order, the Attorney General and the Secretary of Education shall jointly issue guidance regarding the measures and practices required to comply with the Supreme Court's decision in *Students for Fair Admissions, Inc. v. President and Fellows of Harvard College*, 600 U.S. 181 (2023).

Section 5. Ending Illegal Private-Sector DEI Discrimination and Preferences.

(a) Within 120 days of the date of this order, the Attorney General, in consultation with the heads of relevant agencies and in coordination with the Director of the Office of Management and Budget, shall submit a report to the Assistant to the President for Domestic Policy containing recommendations for enforcing Federal civil-rights laws and taking other appropriate measures to encourage the private sector to end illegal discrimination and preferences, including DEI. Such report shall contain a proposed strategic enforcement plan identifying:

(i) The most egregious and discriminatory DEI practitioners in each sector of concern, including publicly traded corporations, large nonprofit corporations or associations, foundations with assets of $500 million or more, State and local bar and medical associations, and institutions of higher education with endowments over $1 billion; and

(ii) A plan of specific steps or measures to deter DEI programs or principles (whether specifically denominated "DEI" or otherwise) that constitute illegal discrimination or preferences.

(b) As part of the strategic enforcement plan required by subsection (a) of this section, the head of each agency shall identify up to nine potential civil compliance investigations of entities listed in subsection (a)(i) of this section.

Section 6. Federal Contracting and Grant Compliance.

The head of each agency shall ensure that every Federal contract or grant award entered into by such agency includes:

(a) A term requiring every Federal contractor or grantee to agree that its compliance in all respects with all applicable Federal anti-discrimination laws is material to the government's payment decisions for purposes of section 3729(b)(4) of title 31, United States Code; and

(b) A term requiring every Federal contractor or grantee to certify that it does not operate any programs promoting DEI that violate any applicable Federal anti-discrimination laws.

Section 7. Exceptions.

(a) Nothing in this order shall be construed to prohibit Federal or private-sector employment and contracting preferences for veterans of the Armed Forces of the United States.

(b) This order does not prevent persons teaching at a Federally funded institution of higher education as part of a larger course of academic instruction from advocating for, endorsing, or promoting the unlawful employment or contracting practices prohibited by this order.

Section 8. General Provisions.

(a) Nothing in this order shall be construed to impair or otherwise affect:

(i) The authority granted by law to an executive department, agency, or the head thereof; or

(ii) The functions of the Director of the Office of Management and Budget relating to budgetary, administrative, or legislative proposals.

(b) This order shall be implemented consistent with applicable law and subject to the availability of appropriations.

(c) This order is not intended to, and does not, create any right or benefit, substantive or procedural, enforceable at law or in equity by any party against the United States, its departments, agencies, or entities, its officers, employees, or agents, or any other person.

Appendix A: President Trump's January 2025 EOs for DEI

Appendix A Notes

1. Donald J. Trump, Executive Order 14151, Ending Radical and Wasteful Government DEI Programs and Preferencing, https://www.federalregister.gov/documents/2025/01/29/2025-01953/ending-radical-and-wasteful-government-dei-programs-and-preferencing, January 20, 2025.

2. Donald J. Trump, Executive Order 14168: "Defending Women from Gender Ideology Extremism and Restoring Biological Truth to the Federal Government," https://www.federalregister.gov/documents/2025/01/30/2025-02090/defending-women-from-gender-ideology-extremism-and-restoring-biological-truth-to-the-federal, January 20, 2025.

3. Trump, Donald J. "Executive Order 14173: Ending Illegal Discrimination and Restoring Merit-Based Opportunity." Federal Register 90, no. 20 (January 31, 2025): 8635-8636. https://www.federalregister.gov/documents/2025/01/31/2025-02000/ending-illegal-discrimination-and-restoring-merit-based-opportunity.

APPENDIX B

14th Amendment to the U.S. Constitution

Section 1.

All persons born or naturalized in the United States, and subject to the jurisdiction thereof, are citizens of the United States and of the State wherein they reside. No State shall make or enforce any law which shall abridge the privileges or immunities of citizens of the United States; nor shall any State deprive any person of life, liberty, or property, without due process of law; nor deny to any person within its jurisdiction the equal protection of the laws.

Section 2.

Representatives shall be apportioned among the several States according to their respective numbers, counting the whole number of persons in each State, excluding Indians not taxed. But when the right to vote at any election for the choice of electors for President and Vice-President of the United States, Representatives in Congress, the Executive and Judicial officers of a State, or the members of the Legislature thereof, is denied to any of the male inhabitants of such State, being twenty-one years of age, and citizens of the United States, or in any way abridged, except for participation in rebellion, or other crime, the basis of representation therein shall be reduced in the proportion which the number of such male citizens shall bear to the whole number of male citizens twenty-one years of age in such State.

Section 3.

No person shall be a Senator or Representative in Congress, or elector of President and Vice-President, or hold any office, civil or military, under the United States, or under any State, who, having previously taken an oath, as a member of Congress, or as an officer of the United States, or as a member of any State legislature, or as an executive or judicial officer of any State, to support the Constitution of the United States, shall have engaged in insurrection or rebellion against the same, or given aid or comfort to the enemies thereof. But Congress may by a vote of two-thirds of each House, remove such disability.

Section 4.

The validity of the public debt of the United States, authorized by law, including debts incurred for payment of pensions and bounties for services in suppressing insurrection or rebellion, shall not be questioned. But neither the United States nor any State shall assume or pay any debt or obligation incurred in aid of insurrection or rebellion against the United States, or any claim for the loss or emancipation of any slave; but all such debts, obligations and claims shall be held illegal and void.

Section 5.

The Congress shall have the power to enforce, by appropriate legislation, the provisions of this article.

Author Bios

Born into abject poverty in rural southwest Virginia, **Dr. Carol Swain**, a high school dropout, went on to earn five degrees. Holding a Ph.D. from the University of North Carolina at Chapel Hill and an M.S.L. from Yale, she also earned early tenure at Princeton and full professorship at Vanderbilt where she was professor of political science and a professor of law. Today she is a sought-after cable news contributor, a best-selling author, a prominent national speaker, and an entrepreneur.

In addition to having three Presidential appointments, Dr. Swain is a former Distinguished Senior Fellow for Constitutional Studies with the Texas Public Policy Foundation. She has also served on the Tennessee Advisory Committee to the U.S. Civil Rights Commission, the National Endowment for the Humanities, and the 1776 Commission. In 2025, she received the Frederick Douglass Lifetime Achievement Award for a lifetime of conservative service to the nation. Currently, she is a senior fellow at the Institute for Faith and Culture.

An award-winning political scientist cited three times by the U.S. Supreme Court, Dr. Swain has authored or edited thirteen published books including the bestseller, *Black Eye for America: How Critical Race Theory is Burning Down the House*. Other books include *The Gay Affair: Harvard, Plagiarism, and the Death of Academic Integrity*; *Countercultural Living: What Jesus Has to Say About Life, Marriage, Race, Gender, and Materialism*; and

The Adversity of Diversity: How the Supreme Court's Decision to Remove Race from College Admissions Criteria will Doom Diversity Programs.

She is an expert on American politics, immigration reform, affirmative action and DEI policies, and evangelical politics. Her television appearances include BBC News, ABC's Headline News, CBS, CNN, Fox News, Newsmax and more. In addition, she has published opinion pieces in the *New York Times*, the *Washington Post*, the *Wall Street Journal*, the *Epoch Times*, the *Financial Times*, and *USA Today*.

Dr. Swain is the founder and CEO of Carol Swain Enterprises, REAL Unity Training Solutions, Your Life Story for Descendants, and her nonprofit, Be the People.

She is a mother, grandmother, and great-grandmother who resides in Nashville, Tennessee.

Mike Towle is a former newspaper reporter, editor, and general manager for publications such as the *St. Albans (Vermont) Messenger*, the *Fort Worth Star-Telegram*, *The National Sports Daily*, and the *Nashville Tennessean*, the latter for which he won six statewide Tennessee Press Association awards in column writing.

Towle has authored or co-authored more than twenty books published by the likes of HarperCollins, Rutledge Hill Press, WND Books, Triumph Books, Cumberland House, and Fitting Press, as well as his own nationally distributed trade imprints TowleHouse Publishing and Win-Win Words.

A native of Vermont, a graduate of the University of Notre Dame, and a former Army officer, Towle resides in the Nashville, Tennessee, area.